LINDA RIOS BROOK

LUCIFER'S WAR

UNDERSTANDING THE ANCIENT STRUGGLE BETWEEN GOD AND THE DEVIL

Why does evil persist?
Where does Satan get his power?
If Satan is defeated, why doesn't he give up?

There are many views concerning Satan and how to fight him and his minions. With great insight Linda Rios Brook has managed to capture golden nuggets that all who desire to know and understand the invisible realms of the spirit world need to grasp.

—JOHN PAUL JACKSON
FOUNDER OF STREAMS MINISTRIES AND AUTHOR OF
NEEDLESS CASUALTIES OF WAR

I have been intrigued by Linda Rios Brook because of her sharp mind and keen business sense. Her latest book will challenge, captivate, provoke, inspire, and maybe even infuriate you. She is a thinker, a seeker, even a provoker. In this book Linda asks the hard questions about evil, God, angels, the power of prayer, spiritual warfare, etc. Though you may not always agree with her answers, you won't be able to put the book down. It is engaging, challenging, and will prod you to think like you've never thought before. I admire her gutsy decision to say it like she thinks it, as well as to tease out truth. This book will make you think and set a correction course for many.

—BARBARA J. YODER
LEAD APOSTLE OF SHEKINAH REGIONAL EQUIPPING
AND REVIVAL CENTER AND AUTHOR OF *TAKING ON
GOLIATH*

Linda Rios Brook is one of our great Christian thinkers who will challenge you to reach beyond common thought to expand your knowledge of the heavenly realm. Provocative and brilliantly researched, *Lucifer's War* not only opens the windows of understanding into the arena of Satanology, but it also showers much needed light on our human position and entitlements and as children of the kingdom of God. An ideal book to share, discuss, and reread many times.

—MARIE CHAPIAN, PhD
NEW YORK TIMES BEST-SELLING AUTHOR OF *ANGELS IN OUR LIVES*, COAUTHOR OF *THE OTHER SIDE OF SUFFERING* (WITH JOHN RAMSEY) AND *THE EMANCIPATION OF ROBERT SADLER* (WITH ROBERT SADLER), AND PULITZER PRIZE AND PUSHCART PRIZE NOMINEE

Lucifer's War gives the best and most concise intellectual and spiritual treatment of the age-old problem of evil vs. good with substantive and in-depth analysis. Many of the questions we have been too timid to answer or research are discussed in this book. Linda Rios Brook deals with the issues of spiritual battle forthrightly by a thorough investigation of Scripture and traditions. You will be enlightened and informed by her definitive and delightful approach. Linda gives a most accurate account of the devil and the intended purposes of mankind and the church. A greater revelation of the cosmic conflict of good and evil is given in a captivating and impressive literary style. So, in Linda's vernacular, "Let the reader beware."

—NORMAN D. BENZ, DMIN
LEAD PASTOR OF COVENANT CENTRE INTERNATIONAL, PALM BEACH GARDENS, FLORIDA

I commend Linda Rios Brook for challenging us to reexamine the interrelationships that exist between the spiritual and natural realms. Through this book we are reminded that "still our ancient foe doth seek to work us woe." Yet we are empowered by the Holy Spirit to be integral agents for light, for truth, and for life. And like it or not, we too are engaged in this warfare. It is a call to arms, not a time to shrink back!

—REV. ROBERT BURMEISTER
ASSOCIATE PASTOR, NORTH HEIGHTS LUTHERAN
CHURCH, ARDEN HILLS, MINNESOTA, AND
FEATURED IN *THE REAL EXORCISTS*, WHICH AIRED
ON THE HISTORY CHANNEL

I have to say this is one of the best books I've ever read—period! *Lucifer's War* is not some work of fiction that offers more fantasy than fact. Neither is it a theological treatise that offers little, if any, practical wisdom. In a way that only someone who has experienced this reality in the real world can communicate, Linda Rios Brook has brought to us a classic work that is both thought-provoking and inspiring, challenging and entertaining, insightful and imaginative. It is a *must*-read for everyone who appreciates questions and answers.

—MARK PFEIFER
FOUNDER AND SENIOR PASTOR, OPEN DOOR
CHRISTIAN FELLOWSHIP, CHILLICOTHE, OHIO
LEAD APOSTLE OF THE SOMA FAMILY OF
MINISTRIES

Linda Rios Brook is a deep thinker and a woman of many gifts and talents. In this book she returns us to more ancient possible thoughts concerning demonic powers, angels, and pre-Adamic beings. While such thoughts were common in ancient times among early Jews and Christians, these types of possibilities have been dismissed by our Western rationalistic culture. Linda Rios Brook is saying not so fast; there is more in the hints in Scripture and ancient texts that should be given a hearing. She makes a significant case that the heavens and the earth, and the seen and unseen, are much bigger than our philosophy allows.

—DANIEL JUSTER, THD
DIRECTOR OF TIKKUN INTERNATIONAL, ISRAEL

We have entered a time of great trouble, with disasters on every side, leading us into the ultimate battle between light and darkness. Where is our Champion-God in all of this? This book from Linda Rios Brook will cause you to rethink some of your age-old perceptions of Satan, angels, and why evil exists in our world. She challenges our familiar stereotypes as she leads us back into the history and root of many of our beliefs, some of which are not even based in Scripture. She has done her research well, presenting to the church of the last days a fascinating and thought-provoking manual that will be read and reread by God's overcomers! Read it and be stretched to see even more of the wisdom of God!

—DR. BRIAN SIMMONS
FOUNDER AND DIRECTOR, APOSTOLIC RESOURCE
CENTER

There's an X factor in the cosmos, and in *Lucifer's War* Linda Rios Brook may have worked through the calculus to isolate it. For centuries thoughtful people have pondered how an all-loving, all-powerful God could allow evil to wreak havoc in His good world. This bold—borderline audaciously bold—book may resolve the riddle, which I won't spoil here. Suffice it to say, I buy her thesis and am honored to urge you to buy the book! More than theological fancy, this book goes further to suggest a hopeful and solidly biblical solution, a war plan of sorts for the church's partnership with the Lord of all the lords in His mission to take back the planet!

—MARK HERRINGSHAW, PHD
SPEAKER AND AUTHOR OF *SIX PRAYERS GOD ALWAYS ANSWERS*, *NINE WAYS GOD ALWAYS SPEAKS*, AND *THE KARMA OF JESUS*

LUCIFER'S
WAR

LUCIFER'S WAR

LINDA RIOS BROOK

CHARISMA
HOUSE

Most CHARISMA HOUSE BOOK GROUP products are available at special quantity discounts for bulk purchase for sales promotions, premiums, fund-raising, and educational needs. For details, write Charisma House Book Group, 600 Rinehart Road, Lake Mary, Florida 32746, or telephone (407) 333-0600.

LUCIFER'S WAR by Linda Rios Brook
Published by Charisma House
Charisma Media/Charisma House Book Group
600 Rinehart Road
Lake Mary, Florida 32746
www.charismahouse.com

Unless otherwise noted, all Scripture quotations are from the New International Version. Copyright © 1973, 1978, 1984, International Bible Society. Used by permission.

Scripture quotations marked KJV are from the King James Version of the Bible.

Scripture quotations marked NAS are from the New American Standard Bible. Copyright © 1960, 1962, 1963, 1968, 1971, 1972, 1973, 1975, 1977, 1995 by the Lockman Foundation. Used by permission. (www.Lockman.org)

Scripture quotations marked THE MESSAGE are from The Message: The Bible in Contemporary English, copyright © 1993, 1994, 1995, 1996, 2000, 2001, 2002. Used by permission of NavPress Publishing Group.

Quotations from the Quran are from The Quran Translation, 7th edition, translated by Abdullah Yusef Ali (Elmhurst, NY: Tahrike Tarsile Quran, Inc., 2001).

Author is represented by the literary agency of Alive Communications, Inc., 7680 Goddard Street, Suite 200, Colorado Springs, CO, 80920.

Cover design by Justin Evans
Design Director: Bill Johnson

Visit the author's website at www.reluctantdemondiaries.com or visit her at Facebook/LindaRiosBrook.

Publisher's Note: Linda Rios Brook is a prolific author who has written a series of novels on the creation of the earth and the war in heaven that led to the fall of Lucifer. She is frequently asked about the spiritual landscape she has drawn in this series, The Reluctant Demon Diaries, and her understanding of Satan's strategy to destroy God's people. This book is her attempt to answer those questions. It comes after many years of extensive research and consultation with leading theologians and prophetic ministers. However, it is not meant to be viewed as theological fact, nor was it written to persuade anyone to change his or her point of view. It reflects the author's own journey to understand Satan's end game and her speculation about why evil seems to persist in the face of fervent prayer.

Library of Congress Cataloging-in-Publication Data:

Brook, Linda Rios.
  Lucifer's war / Linda Rios Brook.
      p. cm.
  Includes bibliographical references (p.   ).
  ISBN 978-1-61638-696-2 (trade paper) -- ISBN 978-1-62136-040-7 (e-book)
  1. Spiritual warfare--Biblical teaching. I. Title.
  BS680.S73B76 2012
  235'.4--dc23

                                   2012023672

First edition

12 13 14 15 16 — 9 8 7 6 5 4 3 2 1
Printed in the United States of America

CONTENTS

Introduction

TELLING OURSELVES THE TRUTH

I FEEL OBLIGATED TO be clear what this book is *not* about. This is not a self-help or a how-to book, and it doesn't offer ten easy steps to anything. While it may raise as many questions as it answers, it intends to address only three: (1) Why does evil persist? (2) If Satan is a defeated enemy, why does it appear as though he is not? and (3) Why does he not give up?

Prior to publishing it, I shared this manuscript with a number of ministers, several theologians and academics, and an exorcist. I was not surprised to find there was no middle ground in what they thought of it. By a large margin most agreed with theologian Gregory A. Boyd, PhD, who wrote me in an e-mail, "I hope this saves the world from a lot of bad theology." But there were also a few who were somewhat distressed by the book's implication: the reason we have made so little progress in ridding the world of evil in all its forms is because to a degree, we have misunderstood who Satan is, *why* he is, and what he remains capable of doing. This would explain why our spiritual warfare tactics seem to yield so few measurable results.

It will not be my intention to explain evil by assigning blame or speculating on the consequences of dysfunctional lifestyles, poor decision making, mental illness, gender identity, pornography, drugs, or addiction as the reason for demonic attacks. Nor will I have much to say about correct doctrine, spiritual maturity or the lack thereof, breaking spiritual bondage, recovery, or living a fuller life of faith. While related to the problem, this book will not be about deliverance from evil spirits. (In my view the best books on that topic have already been written by people such as Doris Wagner, Rebecca Greenwood, Neil Anderson, and Barbara Yoder, among others.)

I hope this book will do more than acknowledge the obvious: that something has gone terribly wrong in the world. Evil rages at an unacceptable level in, around, and against individuals and groups of people who are created in the image of God, and no one appears able to do very much about it.

Something is wrong in the world for which organized religion, philanthropy, generosity, or political strategies do not seem to have an answer. In particular, people of faith should be chagrined that despite billions in foreign missions, and churches, mosques, and synagogues in every city, what used to work, if it ever did, does not seem to work now. Violence and destruction that produce human suffering in many parts of the world are worse, not better.

Something is wrong in places such as Darfur, where the enslavement and slaughter of innocent men, women, and children is beyond the influence of the great nations of the world. Something is wrong in parts of Asia, where growing numbers of girls and boys younger than eleven years old are kidnapped or sold into the sex trade because they are less likely to have AIDS than their teenage siblings. Something is wrong in parts of the Middle East, where human torture draws celebratory crowds. Something is wrong where natural disasters have decimated villages and the lives of people least able to recover from unspeakable loss. Something has gone wrong in America, the Netherlands, Mexico, Central America, Asia, and other parts of the world where the insatiable appetite for illegal drugs resists and thwarts law and order.

Something beyond fatherless homes, colonization, intolerance, Western greed, racism, and religious wars is wrong. Brutality beyond the human capacity to inflict torture has become common. The Catholic church, the charismatic church, the denominational church, the independent church, the evangelical church, the emergent church, or the deep church has not successfully launched a comprehensive assault against what is wrong, and yet the church alone is authorized to deal with the problem at its source (2 Cor. 5:18–19).

If people of faith are to draw a line and say, "This far and no farther," it will require a better understanding of the enemy we face. We are in the midst of an ancient, ongoing, global, celestial struggle for power and authority to govern and control human behavior and subsequently the nations of the earth, even the planet itself. Whether one believes in angels and demons and their interaction with human beings to achieve opposing missions is inconsequential to the fact that they do exist, and they are actively engaged in a war that remains largely unchanged two thousand years after Christ.

Because "what is wrong" is manifested through individuals, we will begin our quest with a look at four stories about ordinary people who awoke one day to find themselves in circumstances they could never have imagined. The first story has a happy ending; the other three do not. But at the end of each, we are left with the same question: why?

Chapter 1

MORE QUESTIONS THAN ANSWERS

LISA HARREL, A postal worker in Albany, New York, was delivering mail to a home late one Monday morning in 2008 when she looked up and noticed a baby in a window above the front door. "The next thing I knew, she had fallen into my arms," Lisa said.

When the baby's mother realized what had happened, she ran outside and grabbed the one-year-old child from Lisa.

The woman thanked her and then ran down the street to her neighbor's house. Paramedics checked the baby at the scene but found no injuries.[1]

How was a potentially fatal accident averted? Some people familiar with the story declared it a miracle. What else could it have been? The timing was precise. If Lisa had been walking down the sidewalk when she saw the baby about to fall instead of standing directly under the window, she would not have had enough time to rush to catch her. Suppose Lisa had already deposited the mail and taken one step off the porch when she heard a noise and turned around? The little girl would have crashed to the concrete steps. If Lisa had been five seconds earlier or later, a tragedy might have occurred. Surely God had intervened.

On a sunny Monday morning in October 2006, a dairy truck driver walked into an Amish schoolhouse set back in a cornfield on a street of stone houses, barns, and silos in Lancaster County, Pennsylvania. Heavily armed, Charles C. Roberts entered the one-room school and ordered the boys and several adults to leave, then demanded that the eleven girls line up facing the blackboard. As Roberts lashed the students' legs together with wire and plastic ties, the teacher fled the room and called the police. By the time the police arrived, the gunman had murdered four girls and wounded several others before killing himself. A fifth child died in a Delaware hospital the following day.[2]

The Amish are a people of simple faith, piety, and prayer, yet no miraculous rescue occurred. Why did God not intervene to spare the innocent children? What do people of faith have to say in response to such a horrific crime? Some have said there are no answers because God's ways are not our ways, but God must have allowed it to happen for a purpose. John Calvin once said, "Anyone who has been taught by Christ's lips...will look farther afield for a cause, and will consider that all events are governed by God's secret plan."[3] What secret plan of God includes the massacre of Amish schoolchildren? Can anyone theorize even one providential reason God thought it better to allow this tragedy than to prevent it?

We will probably never know exactly how the convoy from Blackwater Security Consulting was stopped on April 1, 2004. Some reports suggested the drivers made the fatal mistake of hitting the brakes instead of flooring the accelerator in hopes of barging through the armed men blocking their path. Others speculated the occupants had already been shot dead before their cars came to a stop.

After learning what happened next, the grieving families more than likely hope the latter was the case. In a savage act that is shocking even for blood-soaked Fallujah, the bodies of the occupants inside the vehicles were beaten, burned, and dismembered. But the worst was yet to come. In what turned into a macabre town fete, at least one corpse was tied to a car and pulled triumphantly through the city streets amid a cheering crowd and in full view of a camera crew. The attackers hung two of the charred and mangled corpses from an iron bridge spanning the Euphrates River. "The people of Fallujah hanged some of the bodies on the old bridge like slaughtered sheep," resident Abdul Aziz Mohammed said gleefully.[4]

Do you suppose the families and friends of the men and women assigned to that dangerous part of the world prayed for protection and mercy? Yet no miraculous intervention occurred. Why not? Senseless violence does not increase our confidence in a loving, omnipotent God who could have protected His children from travesty but chose not to do so. Where does a minister find the words to ease the wrenching pain of the wife or mother who has witnessed her husband or son butchered on live television?

"We must believe unquestioningly that...it is pleasing to God to sacrifice ourselves to Him, that it is by His divine Providence that we are abandoned to all kinds of conditions, to suffer all kinds of sufferings, miseries, and temptations," wrote Brother Lawrence.[5] Those who have stood helplessly by and witnessed people being tortured and dismembered are not consoled by religion that insists the butchers could not have inflicted such harm unless God allowed it for a greater purpose. Clichés are no comfort to those caught up in a nightmare.

On January 23, 2002, on his way to what he thought was an interview with Sheikh Mubarak Ali Gilani at the Village Restaurant in downtown Karachi, Pakistan, Daniel Pearl was kidnapped by a militant group calling itself The National Movement for the Restoration of Pakistani Sovereignty. The group claimed Pearl was not a journalist but rather a CIA operations officer and, using a Hotmail e-mail account, sent the United States a range of demands, including the freeing of

all Pakistani terrorist detainees and the release of a US ship-
ment of F-16 fighter jets to the Pakistani government.

The message read: "We give u 1 more day if America will
not meet our demands we will kill Daniel. Then this cycle will
continue and no American journalist could enter Pakistan."
Attached to the message were photos of Pearl handcuffed
with a gun to his head and holding up a newspaper. There
was no response to pleas from Pearl's editor or from his wife,
Mariane.[6]

Nine days later Pearl was beheaded. On May 16 his severed
head and decomposed body were found cut into ten pieces and
buried, along with the jacket of a tracksuit Pearl was wearing
when photographed by his kidnappers, in a shallow grave at
Gadap, located about thirty miles north of Karachi.[7]

For many days during his captivity Pearl was the focus of
countless prayers for his release, yet no divine rescue occurred.
I doubt his grieving wife would have been comforted to know
that all things, evil and despicable as they may be, work
together for the glory of God. What reasonable person would
have the audacity to urge Daniel Pearl's parents to accept the
brutal dismemberment of their son as having come from the
hand of a loving Father? The idea that beheading and unimaginable brutality have a "higher purpose" is insulting to those
who are victims of horror and to the character of God.

How do we explain that the God who so precisely ordered
the footsteps of a civil servant to be in the right spot to catch
a baby falling from a second-story window is the same God
who seemed unmoved by the slaughter of American contractors on a national building assignment or the beheading of
a Jewish journalist on a peace mission? Are we to somehow

rationalize that the murders of schoolgirls are unfortunate but acceptable casualties to test the faith and fortitude of Amish parents so God can be glorified? Is that really the best we can do?

The contradictions and calamities apparent in these stories represent the enigmatic tension of the cosmos. Either God is omniscient, omnipresent, and omnipotent—able to know all things, be all places, and with all sufficient power to rescue us as our creed declares—or He is something else. If what we insist is true of Him really is, then why does He sometimes intervene and sometimes not?

E. Frank Tupper asks the question this way: "If God really has the power to intervene in nature and history whenever, wherever, and however God chooses, why does God not do so? The monarchical model of a do Anything, Anytime, Anywhere kind of God cannot account for the failure of God to act to prevent a colossal catastrophe or to deliver a segment of vulnerable humanity from some monstrous evil."[8]

If it is God's unwavering intent to rescue, redeem, and restore humanity and all creation as Romans 8 declares, then it must be someone else's intent to kill, steal, and destroy them. The aim of this book is to assign the blame for wickedness and all of its manifestations squarely where it belongs—with the archangel named Lucifer, not with God. Yahweh is not the source of horror; Lucifer is. God is not opposed by a force, a philosophy, or bad theology but rather by a powerful evil being that savagely wars against and through flesh and blood, nature, and other supernatural beings to relentlessly oppose God's objective to reconcile His creation to Himself.

Just as the fullness of God was resident in a person, Jesus

(Col. 1:19), the fullness of evil also resides in a person who rages to annul the covenant of redemption between Jesus and all of creation by ruling through and/or destroying humanity. Why? What does Lucifer stand to gain or lose from what happens to people? Everything, because humanity was the game-changer.

THE WAR OF THE ANGELS

In the beginning, before anything that exists ever was, the war in heaven raged between the angels. As this book will reveal, God's sovereign decision to create a self-willed race in His likeness represented a pivotal point in the war of the cosmos.

If we are to prevail against Lucifer's plans to consume and devour the human race, we must understand him better than we do. How did the war start? What is it about? More importantly, is it certain that we win? While it may shatter our illusions, the answer to the last question on so many levels is, "No, it is not certain we will win." The redemption of the human soul by the blood of the Lamb is certain; the fate of the earth and its inhabitants is not.

Gregory A. Boyd, PhD, writes in his book *Satan and the Problem of Evil*: "While Scripture emphasizes God's ultimate authority over the world, it also emphasizes that agents, whom God has created, can and do resist His will. Scripture does not teach that God controls all the behavior of free agents, whether humans or angels. Humans and fallen angels are able to grieve God's Spirit and to some extent frustrate His purpose (Gen. 6:6; Is. 63:10; Luke 7:30; Eph. 4:30; Heb.

3:8, 15; 4:7). While His *general will* for world history cannot fail, His *particular will* for individuals, often does."[9]

While Boyd may help explain why evil things happen, he does not tell us how, or if, we can avoid being among those for whom God's will does not come to pass. Winning this battle requires a paradigm shift in how we understand what in the world is going on. Lucifer is smarter than we think he is. He is willing to change his tactics when necessary. He manifests and masquerades his rage against God in human drama such as rabid intolerance, mental illness, demonic oppression and possession, ethnic wars, violence, brutality, religious fundamentalism, and scores of other ways about which God, at times, seems unwilling or unable to do very much.

FACING THE TRUTH

Does Lucifer know he is defeated? No, he does not. He does not behave as one who knows he is defeated. In any war, when one side recognizes the futility of continuing the battle, that side seeks to minimize its damages. It is willing to make a deal, declare a truce, cut its losses. The insurgent forces against the purposes of God are a kingdom of self-willed, powerful beings organized under Lucifer's leadership that may acknowledge the efficacy of Jesus in saving the souls of people but little else. The war in the heavens that started before creation continues today. The only change is that there is a new player: humanity.

Lucifer was created by God; his power came from God. God's gifts, to humans or angels, are irrevocable whether they are used for good or evil. A talented singer may lead a worship team or a satanic band; it is the same gift. The person with keen spiritual discernment may be a prophet or a psychic; it is the same gift making him or her sensitive to spiritual realities. Lucifer defies Christian clichés that portray him as a "toothless lion devoid of power." If that were so, the world would not look the way that it does. Apartheid, ethnic cleansing, genocide, and slavery would not exist. Two thousand years this side of the cross, Lucifer, now called Satan, continues to assault human beings in monstrous ways and wars against God Himself for the same reason he always has.

He thinks he can win.

Chapter 2

WHEN WAR BROKE OUT IN HEAVEN

ALL HUMANS AND most angels are involved in a cosmic battle against a common enemy. Angels are aware of the conflict; humans, not so much. The fact that many people are uninformed that the struggle, suffering, tragedy, and loss in their lives can to some measure be attributed to a supernatural intelligence poised against them, or leeched from them, does not lessen the fact that it is so.

We do not have to look far for an analogy to which most people can relate. Afghanistan is a nation where, at the time of this writing, armed forces from other countries, including the United States, are engaged in a war on its soil. The question many ask is why. What is to be gained by the extraordinary loss of lives and money in supporting this clash of nations? None of the participants have a plan to capture land in order to build neighborhoods so their citizens can live in Afghanistan. No one has an interest in colonizing the rugged country. There are few, if any, natural resources such as oil reserves to fight over. So what is this war about?

At its root it is an ideological and spiritual war over views about God. While Western nations nervously balk at claims they are fighting over religion, Islamic extremists make no such denials. To each nation involved in the conflict, the small country most people cannot find on a map is seen as one of two things: a haven for global terror operatives or a bastion for Islamic soldiers determined to defeat the infidels.

What about the Afghani citizens caught in the middle of a battlefield? Have they chosen this war? Most Afghanis do not own any weapons, nor do they belong to the military. Although they are the legal occupants of the land, they are powerless to summarily dismiss the armies, demand to be left alone, and send everyone home. Their lives are consumed by conflict they did not invite and for the most part do not understand.

Similarly, there is a battle taking place over Planet Earth between external forces that are not native to the land. The people of the earth did not cause the war, few understand what it is about, and most possess no weapons to defend themselves against the crossfire. The fight is between God and Satan and the lesser celestial beings loyal to each. Unlike the war in Afghanistan, the opposing forces do indeed have a plan for colonization that will determine which kingdom will be established and ultimately rule the planet. Earth people are caught in the midst of the battle and conscripted into service whether or not they believe in the reasons for the conflict.

An ancient struggle that began in heaven moved to a new battlefield when God reset the rules of engagement for how and where it would be fought. He changed the theater of war from the cosmos to the earth. As a result, every person who has ever lived has been drafted into the epic struggle of good against evil where no conscientious objectors are permitted. Both God and Satan intend to win, and each wants and needs the same thing from people to do so: cooperation and obedience.

Satan is bound by the same rules as the Holy Spirit. Whatever he wishes to do in the earth realm, he must do through a human agent (Eph. 6:12). That is why Satan tried to co-opt Adam and Eve rather than destroy them.

How Did the War Begin?

To understand how the celestial battle between God and a being of His own creation began, we must go back in prehistory, before the human story. "In the beginning [*reshiyth*] God created the heavens and the earth" (Gen 1:1). This simple statement is profound despite its brevity, but it also begs a follow-up question: the beginning of what? If we want to understand what the author meant, we must have an understanding of the language in which he was speaking.

Unfortunately, English does not always do justice to terms translated from the complex languages of Greek and Hebrew. For example, the word for *beginning* (*reshiyth*) in Genesis 1:1 and the word for *beginning (arche)* in John 1:1 have very different meanings. *Reshiyth* means "chief among like things; first in similar events," while *arche* means "the essence of being; before anything was." Let me offer an analogy to explain the distinction.

Many people know that I spent more than twenty years in broadcasting. From time to time some young person wants advice on how to break into such a narrow field and will ask me, "What was your first job?" I answer that my first job was in radio. In fact, that is not true. My first job was selling doughnuts door-to-door when I was eight years old. Working in radio would come years later. It is not that I am not proud of my doughnut career, but the person asking the question is interested in how to break into media, not how to start a bakery enterprise.

When I answer that my first job was in radio, I am referring to my first job relevant to the question being asked, not the first job I ever had. With this in mind, we can better understand Genesis 1:1. That verse tells us that whatever God may have been doing before, when it came to creating things, chief among His creation were the heavens and the earth. If the heavens and the earth represented the epitome of God's handiwork, what would we expect them to look like? Surely they would have been ordered, not chaotic, and beautiful.

Although the universe with its complex array of galaxies must have been working just fine when God finished making it, by the time we reach the second verse of Genesis 1, something appears to have gone wrong with the earth: "Now the earth was formless and empty, darkness was over the surface of the deep."

Many scholars have argued that the word *was* is better translated "had become." If this is true, the paradigm and our understanding immediately shift. The earth was created in some other state before it became formless and empty. The world God had fashioned in perfection and in order had somehow fallen into a state of disrepair. We find clues in the translation of the other nouns in verse 2:

- The Hebrew word for "earth" is *erets*. That term is also translated land, country, field, ground, or wilderness.

- The word for "formless" is *tohuw,* which can also mean a wasteland, desolation, a worthless thing, confusion, a wilderness, or an empty place.

- "Empty" is the word *bohuw,* which can also mean a vacuity or an undistinguishable ruin.

Therefore a reasonable translation of Genesis 1:1–2, as evidenced in the Stone edition of *The Chumash* (which includes the Torah), is: "In the beginning of God's creating the heavens and the earth, the earth had become a confused, desolate, empty place; a wilderness."[1]

What if Scripture is telling us that an unknown length of time passed between the first two verses of Genesis during which something terrible happened to the planet? What might have occurred to bring the world to such a ruinous state? Perhaps an asteroid collided with the earth. Certainly this is a legitimate argument and one that helps explain the moon, the death of dinosaurs, and even the origins of Venus, as some astro-scientists have speculated.

Perhaps Genesis 1:1 describes the original creation, while Genesis 1:2 describes the creation after some trauma had come upon it. Genesis 1:3–31 describes (in literal and nonliteral terms) God's work of restoring the earth by refashioning it out of the materials of the previous creation.

Suppose that when God first created the earth, it looked much as it does today: beautiful and perfectly engineered to sustain complex life, a delicate blue and green bauble hanging in the vastness of space, completely different, even by today's knowledge of the universe, from any of the other barren, desolate planets that populate the cosmos. Now suppose that this marvel of environmental genius was created for living things and was filled with them—animals, plants, and as Derek Prince, Greg Boyd, and others have speculated, a pre-Adamic race of people, about whom we will learn more in chapter 3.

While things were going well on earth, something unthinkable was happening in heaven.

> And there was war in heaven. Michael and his angels fought against the dragon, and the dragon and his angels fought back. But he was not strong enough, and they lost their place in heaven. The great dragon was hurled down—that ancient serpent called the devil, or Satan, who leads the whole world astray. He was hurled to the earth, and his angels with him.
>
> —Revelation 12:7–9

For reasons about which we can only speculate, the most powerful archangel, along with one-third of the angelic realm, was cast down in exile and permitted to roam, virtually unopposed, in the perfect world God had created. What would the earth have become under the rage of one whose purpose was to kill, steal, and destroy anything God had made?

Geology is our record that at one time in its history the earth suffered violent earthquakes, volcanoes, tsunamis, an ice age, shifting polar caps, and all manner of turmoil. While some might believe the ruinous state we find described in Genesis 1:2 may have been the result of a naturally occurring environmental holocaust, could it also indicate a supernatural calamity occurred? I would argue that all supernatural events eventually manifest in the appearance of natural circumstances.

There are always those who will see only a natural explanation for life's happenings. For example, suppose two reporters arrived on the scene at the time of Noah's flood. When the earth was completely deluged, imagine what might have happened if both reporters had been doing a live shot from the bow of the ark.

"Tell us what happened," the studio anchorperson says.

"God judged the world," the first reporter answers.

"Really?" The stunned anchor turns to the other reporter. "Is that what you saw? Did God judge the world?"

"Not at all," the other reporter replies. "It just rained a lot."

Which was it, an act of nature or an act of God? While both would be true, how events are interpreted is greatly influenced by the life experience and point of view of the witness. During the reign of the last king of Judah, a young man named Jeremiah looked across time and saw something remarkable. Some have interpreted his vision as a prophecy about the fall of Jerusalem to Babylon, which would occur later in his lifetime.

Even if this were true, what Jeremiah described does not fit what other historical accounts tell us happened during the siege of Jerusalem. Other people of faith, whose point of view does not allow for human beings to foretell future events, might argue that what Jeremiah reported was something from the past, something he knew about because it was part of the oral history of the people. Perhaps it was as far back as the space between Genesis 1:1–2.

> I looked at the earth—it was back to pre-Genesis chaos and emptiness. I looked at the skies, and not a star to be seen. I looked at the mountains—they were trembling like aspen leaves, and all the hills rocking back and forth in the wind. I looked—what's this! Not a man or woman in sight, and not a bird to be seen in the skies. I looked—this can't be! Every garden and orchard shriveled up. All the towns were ghost towns. And all this because of God, because of the blazing anger of God. Yes, this is God's Word on the matter: "The whole country will be laid waste—still it won't be the end of the world."
>
> —JEREMIAH 4:23–27, THE MESSAGE

WHY EARTH?

We see from this passage in Jeremiah that God's anger can be fierce. Knowing this, it would not be hard to imagine that a rebellious archangel might be thrown out of heaven. It is harder to figure why he was thrown to the earth. We can speculate, but that is all we can do because Scripture is silent on God's reasons for casting Lucifer and the rebelling angels to the beautiful earth instead of to one of the tens of thousands of barren, desolate, uninhabitable planets in the universe. Better yet, why not cast him into a lake of fire of everlasting torment and be done with him?

Now imagine that because of Lucifer and his impact the earth Jeremiah saw in his vision, though once lush and magnificent as it is now, had become a confused, desolate, empty place. Then one day, as Genesis 1:2 goes on to say, God decided to set things back in order, so the Spirit of God hovered over the waters that covered the planet. Modern geology will not contest the belief that water once covered the earth. It might, however, argue about the nature of the water.

The early Jews and neighboring nations believed that the earth was founded on "hostile waters," filled with chaotic and rebellious spirits and forces opposed to God.[2] Many times the Old Testament refers to God's reprimand of water, such as in Psalm 104:7: "But at your rebuke the waters fled, at the sound of your thunder they took to flight."

Why would God rebuke an innocuous compound of two parts hydrogen and one part oxygen? The people of antiquity believed God's chastisement was not against the water itself but what was *in* the water. The Spirit of God not only hovered over the chaos and desolation the earth had become, but specifically over the water where evil beings had taken refuge.

In Genesis 1:3 God said, "Let there be light," and there was light. The Hebrew word *'owr*, which is translated "light," is used in the Old Testament to communicate much more than the difference between day and night. It is commonly used to mean life, happiness, and prosperity. A prominent metaphorical meaning is instruction. While darkness is associated with folly, destruction, suffering, and sin, 'owr is used 120 times in the Old Testament to convey salvation, prosperity, and wisdom.[3]

In the midst of the anarchy Lucifer wreaked upon the earth, the Spirit of God brooded. He rebuked the hostile, demon-filled waters, and the demonic spirits fled. The light—which was the knowledge, wisdom, and salvation of God—pierced the darkness and separated itself from the chaos, confusion, and devastation. And in that place the Lord God planted a garden—and brought forth a new race He named mankind (Adam). Male and female He created them; then He instructed them to fill the earth and subdue it. But subdue it from what?

Genesis makes a point of saying that what God created was good and very good. If there was nothing hostile in what God had made, commanding mankind to subdue it seems a bit over the top. Animals and botanicals alone would not constitute much of a challenge for a new creation in the image of God. God's later command to cultivate the earth and take care of it would have been sufficient unless something opposed to God's intention for mankind was also in Eden.

The purpose for this new race was much more than caretaking. They were to take dominion over—to bring into order and submission—whatever had made the earth a ruinous, desolate, empty wilderness. In other words, they were to curtail the exploits of Satan. The purpose of humankind beginning with Adam and Eve was to refute Satan's intent to govern the earth. *Then something else went wrong.*

Every child in Sunday school learns that Satan, in the guise of a serpent, seduced Adam and Eve to eat from the only tree they were commanded to avoid. What Sunday school fails to teach is the real reason they ate from the tree. They could not have been hungry; they lived in a garden where food was abundant. Why would they disregard the only restriction imposed on them? The conventional responses are that they were proud, they wanted to live forever, or they wanted to be like God, and while those reasons may be true, they are far too simplistic.

Adam and Eve were already like God, and since they had never experienced death, they would have assumed they would live forever; the promise of eternal life would have held no special allure for them. Mankind, both male and female, was fatally compromised for another reason. They underestimated the one who had once been the light-bearer of heaven. They thought he was only a serpent.

Words matter. Since Scripture does not use the word *tempted* in describing Eve's encounter with the serpent, let us not use it either. To do so minimizes the dynamic of what would turn out to be a universe-altering decision. The desire or need to eat forbidden food would have occurred only in response to the body's perception of deprivation. How likely is it that two people who lived in the midst of an orchard would have been willing to take such an enormous risk for a piece of fruit? Eve was not tempted to disobey God; she was beguiled by the charisma of the serpent.

Satan was simply smarter than they thought he was. He

was disarming. He appeared as a creature over which they were confident of their superior status. As a result, the human race, specifically created to subdue evil, lost its first spiritual challenge, and the earth would remain under the dominion of the one known as Satan for thousands of years. While Adam and Eve experienced consequences for what they did, God's wrath was never directed at them. He held Satan explicitly responsible for what had occurred. God would have the last word.

> And I will put enmity between you and the woman, and between your offspring and hers; he will crush your head, and you will strike his heel.
>
> —GENESIS 3:15

The Hebrew word for "head" is *rosh,* which refers to authority. Yahweh's prophecy to the serpent was fulfilled centuries later when Jesus came to do what Adam failed to accomplish. Jesus crushed Satan's head—his authority—but not his power. He could have done that, but He did not. If Jesus had rendered Satan impotent as some Christians insist, the cosmic war would have been over and the New Testament would have ended with the Gospel of John. There would have been no point in going further. When evil is not an option, good men everywhere will obey the law of God written on their hearts (Rom. 2:14).

Why does evil persists two thousand years after the cross? Because Satan is smarter than we think he is and as powerful as he ever was.

Chapter 3

THE DISTURBING CASE OF JOB

MANY PEOPLE THINK Satan cares more about stealing their souls than he does. While there are individuals who may be worthy of his attention, as were Job, Adam, Paul, Peter, and Jesus, most of us are of very little interest to the prince of darkness. Just as Goliath resented the fact that Israel sent a mere boy out to do battle with him, Satan considers men, and especially women, to be inferior creatures and may feel insulted that he has to deal with us at all. Since

God has delegated the affairs of the earth to mankind, the devil has no choice but to confront and co-opt humans if he hopes to thwart God's ultimate plan. Satan does not consider himself to be a defeated enemy, especially as it concerns flesh and blood.

So is Satan's goal to see humans burn in hell? Probably not, if by that we mean he has some interest in what happens to people after their earthly existence is over. Whatever one's theology of heaven and hell, humans are of no benefit to the father of lies after they die, which is why he did not try to kill Adam and Eve. A popular misconception is that Satan rules in hell, where lost souls serve him in never-ending agony. While Michelangelo and Dante might have had such a vision, the writers of the Bible did not. Scripture does not support the notion that lost souls will worship and serve Satan after death. Whatever reality hell may be, Satan is sentenced there as a prisoner himself, not as a ruler. His interest in people is limited to what they can help him accomplish while they are on the earth because they are of no value to him after death.

Some might argue that those who have believed and accepted Jesus are lost to the devil and therefore cannot be manipulated by him. I suggest it is of little concern to Satan what one believes about Jesus so long as he or she can still be useful in his plan to steal, kill, and destroy. Unfortunately, many people have committed Lucifer-inspired acts of violence and injustice while firmly believing they were serving the purposes of God. People who, in the name of Christ, have been complicit in bombing medical facilities or killing doctors and innocent people where abortions are involved come to mind.

Neither biblical authors nor Jesus wrestled with the notion that Satan is anything other than an identifiable being whose intent was and is to frustrate the plans of God by corrupting and impeding the progress of humans as they work to advance the kingdom God intends to establish on the earth. Satan is against us in our endeavor, but his war is with God, not with us.

If God has ordained us to carry out His plans against the devil's counterplans, why is it so hard? "The call of God does not take us where the grace of God cannot keep us," declares the banner of a popular ministry website. "Resist the devil and he will flee," Scripture assures us. Unfortunately this does not appear to be as simple as it sounds. If it were, there would be no martyrs, no injustice, and none of the horrific violence that often befalls righteous people.

Judaism, Islam, and Christianity all declare that God can and will intervene in our circumstances when evil overwhelms us. This belief is the motivation behind most prayer: "God, help us because You can, we cannot, and we are in trouble." This confidence in God's willingness to act on our behalf against evil is a pillar of our faith and is supported by a preponderance of Bible verses. That is, until we get to the Book of Job, a story that should be deeply disturbing to intellectually honest people.

> One day when the angels came to report to God, Satan, who was the Designated Accuser, came along

with them. God singled out Satan and said, "What have you been up to?"

Satan answered God, "Going here and there, checking things out on earth."

God said to Satan, "Have you noticed my friend Job? There's no one quite like him—honest and true to his word, totally devoted to God and hating evil."

(Oh, my, let us stop right here a moment and gasp. Did God really point out Job, someone in whom, up to this point, Satan had taken no notice? Back to the story.)

Satan retorted, "So do you think Job does all that out of the sheer goodness of his heart? Why, no one ever had it so good! You pamper him like a pet, make sure nothing bad ever happens to him or his family or his possessions, bless everything he does—he can't lose! But what do you think would happen if you reached down and took away everything that is his? He'd curse you right to your face, that's what."

God replied, "We'll see. Go ahead—do what you want with all that is his. Just don't hurt him." Then Satan left the presence of God.

—Job 1:6–12, The Message

Don't hurt him? Really? Before the story is completed, Job will have lost all his children and all his wealth and found himself covered with boils. How would a reasonable person understand "don't hurt him"?

While some Bible teachers avoid the Book of Job altogether, most who take it on interpret the passages in an odd way that attempts to placate our sense of justice with conclusions that are frustrating. "In the end, all is well because God repays Job with greater wealth and more children," they say.

Never mind Job's lost crops, animals, and wealth. Material prosperity, however it is defined, is always in a state of flux no matter what one's station in life. Let us talk about the children. Would we seriously suggest this story has a happy ending because Job had more children? Do the new offspring somehow compensate for the loss of the other children?

Thirty-eight years ago two of my dear friends lost their eighteen-month-old son Jeremiah in an unfortunate choking accident. Over the years God blessed them with three more boys who have brought them much joy and pride, but not one of the additional sons has ever remitted the grief of the loss of their firstborn. Knowing Jeremiah is in heaven or that the other sons are prosperous and well does little to stop the tears that flow every year on his birthday.

How can people of faith be taken seriously if we proclaim that every life is unique and purposefully created by God and then sigh with relief because at the end of Job's trials everything worked out just fine? The implied message is that the first generation of children was dispensable and replaceable. Not only is this message inconsistent with our other ideas about God's justice, but it is also abhorrent to people who have experienced the deaths of their own children. If this isn't the intended moral of Job, what is?

Some scholars contend that Job is a mythical character and his story ought not to be taken literally. They cite the fact that there are similar myths in other ancient religions. This is also true of the accounts of Adam and Eve and Noah's ark. The fact that the stories are repeated and mediated through the languages and cultures of many extinct nations does not detract from their authenticity or historical relevance. It only means the stories were well known.

Others insist that Job was a real person who was a contemporary with Abraham. His unfortunate circumstances represented the fruitless struggle of mankind against evil. Therefore God's response to Job's plight was to call Abraham to separate a people unto Himself to become an army against evil. I suggest another possibility. Job was not a contemporary of Abraham but was in fact much older. If this is true, it could mean there is something important about the struggle between God and Satan and human suffering that we have overlooked in Job's story.

"One day the angels came to present themselves before the LORD, and Satan also came with them" (Job 1:6). We should find this disturbing on several levels. When did this meeting take place? It can only be after Satan rebelled and was cast out of heaven; otherwise the fact that he was present with the other nameless angels would be unremarkable. We know the timeline because, if for no other reason, he is referred to as Satan, a name change that came about after his fall from grace. How could it be that an exiled archangel still had access to the counsel of God?

"The LORD said to Satan, 'Where have you come from?'" (v. 7). Why did God ask Satan where he had been? It could not be because He did not know. Just as when God called out to Adam, "Where are you?", it was not because He had misplaced him but because He intended to engage Adam in a deeper discussion. Satan answered that he had been going "here and there over the earth." (See verse 7.) If this answer had been a surprise to God because He had really not kept up with the whereabouts of such a powerful rebel, would it not have been a good time to divert Satan's attention away from the earth, particularly from His righteous servant Job?

Instead, God pointed Job out: "Have you noticed my friend Job? There's no one quite like him—honest and true to his word, totally devoted to God and hating evil" (v. 8, THE MESSAGE).

Up to this point Satan had given Job no particular attention because he must have assumed him to be under God's protection. When God boasted about His faithful servant, Satan challenged Job's motives. "But what do you think would happen if you reached down and took away everything that is his? He'd curse you right to your face, that's what" (v. 11, THE MESSAGE).

When challenged about the reason for Job's loyalty, it seems God agreed to allow Satan to attack Job in brutal ways. No matter which translation of the Bible you might choose, it is almost impossible to read any other interpretation of this conversation. But why? What could God hope to gain by allowing such a confrontation?

It is unimaginable that God had something to prove to Satan by taking him up on a dare. Neither could it have been a test of Job's character. Scripture is clear that Job was a righteous man who hated evil, prayed constantly, and lived a life pleasing to God. When Satan was allowed to attack him, Job was bewildered and undone by the circumstances he found himself in and explicitly held God responsible for what had happened to him.

> What's the point of life when it doesn't make sense, when God blocks all the roads to meaning? Instead of bread I get groans for my supper, then leave the table and vomit my anguish. The worst of my fears has come true, what I've dreaded most has happened. My repose is shattered, my peace destroyed. No rest for me, ever—death has invaded life.
>
> —JOB 3:23–26, THE MESSAGE

And so it goes for the next thirty or so chapters as Job's friends, who are also befuddled by what has happened, try to explain the universal law of cause and effect, insisting that despite his protests of innocence, Job can only be in such a plight because of his sin. And why would they think anything else? The alternative was unbearable. If God would allow such carnage in Job's life without reason, what was to keep something similar from happening to them?

After all the arguments between Job and his friends are exhausted, Job turns his frustration to God. Whether he expected an answer or not, he got one.

> And now, finally, God answered Job from the eye of a violent storm. He said: "Why do you confuse the issue? Why do you talk without knowing what you're talking about? Pull yourself together, Job. Up on your feet! Stand tall! I have some questions for you, and I want some straight answers. Where were you when I created the earth? Tell me, since you know so much!"
>
> —JOB 38:1–4, THE MESSAGE

Many commentators describe God's response as a rebuke of Job's legitimate complaint about his circumstances. I suggest another interpretation is possible. What if God were not saying, "How dare insignificant *you* question omniscient *Me*?" Suppose instead God used the tone of voice one might find in a conversation between a war-weary general and a trusted foot soldier? "I feel your pain, Job, but let Me explain to you how complicated this situation is. From your point of view, you cannot possibly understand what is really at stake."

Theologian Edmond Jacob describes it like this: "God wants to show Job how difficult the conduct of the world is with creatures so extraordinary and so mysterious which fear nothing...and against which He has to wage incessant war. By transposing that [battle] to his own plane, Job will be able to draw the conclusion...that God is not unjust by His lack of concern for him since He Himself on a much higher plane struggles against evil."[1]

After God overwhelms Job with the complexity of creation, He gets to the point. Something evil and dangerous is loose in the world, and one of its manifestations is Leviathan.

> His pride is invincible....Even angels run for cover when he surfaces, cowering before his tail-thrashing turbulence.... There's nothing on this earth quite like him.
>
> —Job 41:15, 25, 33, The Message

Whatever Leviathan was, apparently no one on the earth or in the angelic realm was a match for him. God provided a lengthy and detailed description of what the world was like so Job would realize his own ignorance in understanding the complexity of creation and his and his friends' arrogance in thinking they could trace every horrible thing back to God or human sin. While Job—and we—might have an expanded appreciation of God's grandeur and the involvedness of the universe and its inhabitants, that still does not help us with an indelicate question: Why did God not only allow Satan to attack Job, a righteous man, but also why does it seem that God Himself was the instigator?

Scholar Spiros Zodhiates writes: "The exact time [of Job] is unknown, but many believe that Job lived at the time of Abraham, in the Patriarchal Age. Nowhere is the Law of Moses or the nation of Israel mentioned. The Book of Job was an early part of the wisdom literature of the Old Testament, but it was not connected to Psalms, Proverbs, Song of Solomon, Ecclesiastes, or any other biblical book."[2]

Other scholars argue that the writing of the Book of Job predates the writing of the Book of Genesis. Let us imagine for a moment that the reason Job the book was written first is because Job the man lived before Adam. What if before Adam there was a time when Satan roamed unabated about the earth to which he had been cast down (Rev. 12:9), and, as many have speculated, there also existed a race of people about whom the Bible has nothing to say except that the children of Adam and Eve eventually married some of them? Could it be that Adam and Eve were the second act of human creation and not the first?

ACKNOWLEDGING EVIDENCE

Archeological remains testify to the existence of ancient people groups who lived on the earth as early as forty thousand years ago, predating Jewish history as recorded in the Torah by thousands of years. Though separated by time and geography, all of these races of antiquity shared a similar demise. They disappeared suddenly in unexplained circumstances, but they left artifacts that have helped us piece together what their lives may have been like, allowing us to understand how the world might have been in a much earlier time. If we are willing to look through the framework of discoverable history, we may be able to gain even keener insights into what the biblical record is trying to tell us. Unfortunately, all too often the fields of science and religion have considered themselves mutually exclusive, with no common framework for collaboration.

When my son, Chris, was working on his doctoral dissertation at Baylor University, I became familiar with the concept of complementarity, which was developed through the work of Danish physicist Neils Bohr. Bohr attempted to explain how mutually exclusive sets of experimental data could be equally true though seemingly contradictory.[3] The models through which the information is examined determine its conclusion. For example, light can be observed either as a wave or as particle-like aspects but not both at the same time. Neither method disproves the validity of the other.

Scientist Donald M. MacKay helped popularize this concept, with the central message that "scientists looked at the world as a self-consistent, closed physical system and attempted to understand that world on its own terms. Christians looked at the world as an open system with more processes and events occurring than meet the scientific eye. Only when one accepted the validity of both perspectives could one avoid the potential conflict between them."[4]

In his 1952 BBC address MacKay emphasized that only by

making use of the complementarity concept could one arrive at the fullest understanding of the world: "To keep scientific and Christian doctrines rigidly apart would be silly as well as potentially dishonest. To try to make them into one by chopping bits from each and pasting them together, or by treating them as rival ways of giving identical information, would be equally to miss the point. We can come to relate them properly only by holding both constantly together in our minds, until little by little there comes to us some glimmering of that greater whole of which they present complementary aspects, the activity and character of God himself: not God seen only in the gaps of the scientific picture, not God deduced only as the conclusion of a scientific argument, but God revealed as the Author of the whole story."[5]

Thus complementarity not only justifies the Christian and scientific views of the world, but it also makes proper interaction between them possible.

Before Adam?

In March 1994 some spelunkers exploring an extensive cave system in northern Spain noticed two human mandibles jutting out of the sandy soil. In short order they realized the significance of the find, and with the help of law enforcement they shoveled out more than 140 bones. The fossilized remains are believed to be Neanderthals who lived approximately 43,000 years ago. Analysis of the DNA of the bones would add to speculative research of the past 150 years that present-day people were not the first human-type race to have lived on Planet Earth.

Scientists found the specimen's DNA "differed from living

humans to a degree suggesting that the Neanderthal and modern human lineages had begun to diverge long before the modern human migration out of Africa."[6] Svante Paabo, formerly at the University of Munich, dropped a genetic bombshell when he confirmed that Neanderthals were a separate species from modern human beings. If chimpanzees and humans share a genetic code that is 98.5 percent identical, then Neanderthals and humans would be alike 99.5 percent of the time. The .5 percent variance makes all the difference.

I believe what the archeological findings tell us is that when our ancestors Adam and Eve emerged, they found the landscape already inhabited. Reporting on the find for *National Geographic*, author Stephen S. Hall wrote, "So, while the new genetic evidence appears to confirm that Neanderthals were a separate species from us, it also suggests that they may have possessed human language and were successful over a far larger sweep of Eurasia than previously thought. Which brings us back to the same hauntingly persistent question that has shadowed them from the beginning: Why did they disappear?"[7]

Suppose it was during a span of history about which Scripture has little to say, a time when perhaps Job lived, a time pre-Genesis, perhaps 43,000 years ago when a pre-Adamic race that no longer exists inhabited the earth. How might our understanding of the story change? If Job belonged to a race of people with a .5 percent variance in genetic makeup from Adam's race, might there also have been a similar variance in his spiritual capacity? The world Job lived in was chaotic and overrun by warring factions both natural and supernatural, the chief of which was a ferocious entity named Leviathan. Job's race was no match for what the world had become.

According to the Bible's description concerning Leviathan, he was so powerful that neither angels nor men could subdue him. If God's plans for the earth were to triumph over Satan's plans to rule it, a new response to evil would be needed.

> When God created the human race, he made it godlike, with a nature akin to God. He created both male and female and blessed them, the whole human race.
>
> —GENESIS 5:1–2, THE MESSAGE

THE .5 PERCENT DIFFERENTIAL— THE DNA OF GOD?

Adam was created in the image of God, imbued with the power and authority of God over the land and all that dwelt upon it. Dare we consider that perhaps Job, for whatever reason, was not? Among scholars who argue that the mystery of Job should be regarded as more than an illustration of human suffering is Hugh Ross, PhD, a Canadian-born astrophysicist and Christian apologist who leads a ministry called Reasons to Believe. In a review of Ross's *Hidden Treasures in the Book of Job*, Arthur Khachatryan writes:

> Dr. Ross argues quite persuasively based on inclusions of specific information and omissions of certain others, that Job was most likely the first book of the Bible to be penned, even before Genesis. As such, Job is well suited to provide details to fill in the gaps of the creation account in Genesis about the natural history of

the world. In fact, he argues very persuasively that the gaps in the creation account of Genesis are not really gaps, but exclusions of what would have already been common knowledge because the content of the Book of Job was already familiar to Moses when the Book of Genesis was penned.[8]

It is generally accepted that the order of placement of the books of the Old Testament was not canonized until A.D. 90 at the Council of Jamnia. If Job, the oldest book of the Bible, had been placed in front of Genesis, would we understand the story a different way?

Neither Scripture nor science allows us to say with certainty that a pre-Adamic race of people existed, though there has long been speculation among theologians and Bible teachers such as the late Derek Prince (*War in Heaven*) and Don Basham (*Deliver Us From Evil*) that there may have been such a race. But by considering Job before Genesis in history, might we eliminate the troubling contradiction for many between a seemingly capricious god who seems willing to bargain with the devil using humans as pawns and the Father God of the Bible, who indwells and empowers people to stand against and overcome evil in all of its manifestations? Should not the message of Job be something more than a lesson in sticking it out in the face of relentless assault emanating from a supernatural evil?

Why do we not see God instructing Job to subdue Leviathan and rule over him? Could it be that whoever Job was and however he came to be, he was not a match for the serpent? A different response to evil was needed. Adam, the son of God (Luke 3:38), was able to overcome what Job could not—the serpent. But Adam did not. Adam failed. Jesus, the Son of God and second Adam (1 Cor. 15:45), was needed as God's ultimate remedy to redeem and empower the race of Adam and Eve to achieve its original purpose.

Jesus Shifted the Balance of Power Again

Some argue that Jesus brought only one new ministry to the earth—the power to cast out demons. While the Jews of the first century were familiar with and practiced the rite of exorcism, not many aspired to the calling. Prior to Jesus the method of ridding a person of a demon was for the exorcist to invite the demon to inhabit his own body, usually with devastating consequences to the exorcist, as evident in what happened to the sons of Sceva (Acts 19).

As spectacular as the miracles of Jesus might seem to us, neither healing nor raising the dead were new ideas in the first century. The prophets before Jesus healed through supernatural means and on at least one occasion raised a widow's son after he died. The fact that Jesus could do such things as well was marveled at and deeply appreciated but was not outside the religious paradigm of believing Jews. However, Jesus scandalized the entire religious establishment when He cast out demons by simply telling them to leave then instructing His disciples to do likewise.

After settling the accounts with Satan, Jesus sent the Holy Spirit to permanently reside within human beings to enable them to follow His commandment: "Heal the sick, raise the dead, cleanse those who have leprosy, drive out demons" (Matt. 10:8). For the first time in human history, ordinary people were empowered to contend against the plans of a supernatural being.

As the disciples were, so we are spiritually empowered beyond Adam and beyond Job. But there are parameters to our spheres of authority, and there are great risks in stepping beyond them.

Chapter 4

THE WATCHERS

THERE IS AN ancient Jewish night prayer that says, "May Michael be at my right hand, Gabriel at my left, before me Uriel, and behind me, Raphael, and above my head the divine presence of God."[1] Before Jesus interrupted history, people knew they lived in the midst of a cosmic battle zone between the one true God and a cadre of lesser but still powerful rebellious powers. They also knew there was very little they could do about it. How were mortals expected to withstand attacks by the supernatural? If the righteousness of Job was not sufficient to quell Leviathan, what hope was there for anyone else?

Today Christians believe that our situation is significantly changed from that of Job and Adam, not only through the redemption of Jesus but also because Jesus opened the way for the Holy Spirit to become a permanent resident on the earth by residing in temples of flesh and blood. The balance of supernatural power has shifted. We can now be agents through which God can accomplish His work on the earth regardless of the spiritual resistance that may be set against us. Our confidence comes from the assurance that the Holy Spirit dwells within us and He who is within us is greater than the spiritual forces that oppose us. This is, however, historically speaking, a rather modern event.

All people of antiquity, including the Jews, believed there was an intermediary agency—angels—between humans and God. Before a change in translation between Hebrew and Greek, the Jewish Scriptures described how powerful angels, often referred to as sons of god, were set as guardians over nations. These beings, however, later lost their position because they wanted the humans to worship them. How did this happen?

Some scholars argue that when God created the earth, His original intention was to set governing angels over the nations for the purpose of helping humans. This belief has its origins in Deuteronomy 32:7–9, which the Septuagint (the Greek version of the Old Testament) translates this way: "Remember the days of old, consider the years for past ages....When the Most High divided the nations, when he separated the sons of Adam, he set the bounds of the nations *according to the number of the angels of God*" (emphasis added).

In other words, the division and geographical boundaries of nations were not random but in accordance with the number of high-ranking angelic beings available to oversee and assist the development of humanity. The New Testament agrees with this belief. "Why the Law then? It was added because of transgressions, having been ordained through angels by the agency of a mediator, until the seed would come to whom the promise had been made" (Gal. 3:19, NAS).

FINGERPRINTS OF THE GODS

The remnants and records of all known ancient civilizations have produced an oddly similar mythology of religion whereby the people were helped by one or more superhuman beings. Archaeology has provided us with evidence of many such societies, but none is more fascinating than that of the ancient Egyptians.

Egypt's culture did not emerge into history slowly and painfully as is normal with human societies. Noted archaeologist and scholar Graham Hancock writes: "They emerged all at once and fully framed. Indeed, the period of transition from primitive to advanced society appears to have been so short that it makes no kind of historical sense. Technological skills that should have taken hundreds or even thousands of years to evolve were brought into use almost overnight—and with no apparent antecedents whatever. . . . What is remarkable is there are no traces of evolution from simple to sophisticated, and the same is true of mathematics, medicine, astronomy, and architecture and of Egypt's amazingly rich and convoluted religio-mythological system. How does a complex civilization spring full-blown into being?"[2]

Hancock goes on to present an interesting analogy. "Compare a 1905 automobile to a modern one. There is no mistaking the process of development. But in Egypt, there are no parallels. Everything is right there from the start."[3]

Patrick Heron, author of *The Nephilim and the Pyramid of the Apocalypse*, writes: "Of all the places where the gods of old left their fingerprints Egypt is probably the most pronounced. In fact, not only did they leave their fingerprints, but also their wardrobes, diaries, photo albums, religious rituals, and architecture."[4]

Sadly, none of these civilizations of antiquity have survived. Each of them suddenly and mysteriously disappeared. The squalor and poverty that is prevalent in Cairo today, where hundreds of thousands of people huddle together in cardboard shacks, is not the same society that built the pyramids and ruled the ancient world. Something changed, and while theories abound, no one can say with certainty what happened or why.

The controversial speculation about alien assistance in the construction of some of the architectural wonders of the earth is not so far removed from the biblical idea of high-ranking angels having been assigned by God to help people take dominion over the planet. If that were true, what would explain Egypt's sudden and irreversible fall from grandeur to social degradation?

Perhaps it had something to do with the rebellion of the governing angels. Theologian Greg Boyd writes, "For if and when these guardian angels decide to turn evil, the authority and responsibility given to them is not (cannot be?) immediately retracted. As in the case with human parents and their children, when these angels fall everything they are guardians of suffers accordingly."[5]

The oldest surviving people group with a continuous record of their historical interaction with God and angels are the Jews. After Christianity became the official religion of Rome under Constantine around A.D. 300, the church found itself struggling with the demands of legitimacy.

During this time certain supernatural aspects of the faith, including Jewish beliefs concerning angelology, became an embarrassment to the early church fathers, who were eager to find areas of compromise with the Hellenistic culture. Certain passages of Scripture were simply changed to be more compatible with Greek thinking. Subsequent translations from the Septuagint made a notable change to Deuteronomy 32:8: "When the Most High gave the nations their inheritance, when he divided all mankind, he set up boundaries for the peoples *according to the number of the sons of Israel*" (emphasis added).

In other words, the scriptural declaration that the nations of the earth corresponded to "the number of the angels," as we saw in the translation from the Septuagint, was simply changed to say the nations corresponded to "the number of the sons of Israel." Therefore the ancient belief in the influence of territorial angels as superintendents over the progress of nations has been largely lost in the church age.

If it is true that God's original intention included angels as guardians over nations, did something go wrong? Yes, it did.

A fatal attraction developed. The proclivity of man to seek a mediator between himself and God, combined with the ambition resident in the angelic realm, may have created a perfect environment for unfortunate choices by both. Man's reluctance to approach God directly is at least as old as the Exodus.

Despite the miracles of their deliverance from Egypt and Yahweh's unmistakable provision for them in the desert, the Hebrews remained reluctant to call on God directly, insisting that Moses do it for them.

> Go near and listen to all that the LORD our God says. Then tell us whatever the LORD our God tells you. We will listen and obey.
>
> —DEUTERONOMY 5:27

The New Testament tells us the only mediator between believers and God the Father is Jesus. "For there is one God and one mediator between God and men, the man Christ Jesus" (1 Tim. 2:5). Nonetheless, the ancient belief that other venerated spiritual authorities have influence with God in the lives of ordinary people remains a pillar of the largest church denomination in the world: the Roman Catholic church.

As a general rule, Catholics do not find it odd or inconsistent with faith to ask departed saints or the mother of Jesus herself to intervene on their behalf in a petition to her Son. Indeed, it is commonly believed that particular saints have special areas of authority over nations, vocations, and other categories of life. For example, St. Anthony is the finder of lost objects.[6] St. Fiacre watches over gardeners.[7] St. Adalbert of Prague is the patron saint of Poland[8] and Ansgar over Denmark.[9] St. Vincent de Paul has charge over caregivers, charities, hospitals and hospital workers, lepers, orphans, the poor, prisoners, and volunteers.[10]

There are hundreds more. Despite the objections of Protestants, the Catholic practice of petitioning help from someone in the supernatural realm has its root in one of the earliest books of the Old Testament. The proclivity of people to find an intermediary between themselves and God may have carried over from the interaction between early mankind and the angels who were set as guardians over the nations.

Whatever assignments the angels might have been given by Yahweh concerning the nations, they were never intended to become proxy gods who received worship. But they may have inadvertently become so as a result of people seeking their intervention to attain God's favor and being willing to offer sacrifices and adoration to get it. If ambition was the cause of Lucifer's rebellion against God as some interpret Ezekiel 28:11–15 to say, why would we think other angels might somehow be immune to the seduction of receiving worship?

Let me offer an analogy. Twenty-first-century Western culture is often lamented for abandoning restraint in our devotion to entertainment and sports stars, many of whom succumb to the pressure of what amounts to worship and end up spending years in rehab. Some recover; some do not. Neither people nor angels are psychologically or emotionally wired to become objects of worship. Yet the adoration by others is breathtaking, and those who have experienced it will sometimes resort to bizarre behaviors to retain it. Satan was willing to exchange his legal hold on the world if Jesus would only submit to worship him one time (Luke 4:5–7), a stunning example of the powerful desire for adulation.

Bible scholar D. S. Russell explains it this way: "These gods were never intended to become objects of worship and when they become such objects (perhaps through their own fallen initiative...), they are no longer regarded as legitimate 'sons of God' but as 'demons'.... Their role was to oversee the welfare of the nation assigned to them, not to become surrogate objects of devotion for the Lord himself. When they fail in this duty, they become evil and are judged."[11]

Instead of being agents to serve the purposes of God for the benefit of mankind, they began to mistreat humans, showing favor to those who worshipped them and bringing despair on those who would not. Psalm 82 calls them to task.

> God presides in the great assembly;
>   he gives judgment among the "gods":
> "How long will you defend the unjust
>   and show partiality to the wicked? Selah.
> Defend the cause of the weak and fatherless;
>   maintain the rights of the poor and oppressed.
> Rescue the weak and needy;
>   deliver them from the hand of the wicked.
> They know nothing, they understand nothing.
>   They walk about in darkness;
>   all the foundations of the earth are shaken.
> I said, 'You are "gods";
>   you are all sons of the Most High.'
> But you will die like mere men;
>   you will fall like every other ruler."
>
> —PSALM 82:1–7

If one interprets these verses in the simplest terms possible—in other words, the words mean what they *appear* to mean without passing them through a particular doctrinal screen—it is difficult to draw any other reasonable interpretation except that God Himself is chastising the "gods" or the disobedient angels (demons) for their treatment of human beings they were supposed to help.

Whatever may have transpired in prior centuries, by the time Jesus appeared on the earth, it was widely believed that demons tormented human beings. In fact, one may argue on the basis of the New Testament that the only new ministry Jesus demonstrated was deliverance from evil spirits. In his book *God at War* Greg Boyd quotes author James Kallas as saying, "The arrival of the kingdom is simultaneous with, dependent upon, and manifested in the routing of demons."[12] Boyd goes on to say, "For Jesus, healings, exorcisms clearly did not merely *symbolize* the kingdom of God they *were* the kingdom of God."[13] While healing the sick, cleansing lepers, and raising the dead may have been dazzling to witness, the prophets who preceded Jesus were on record as having accomplished all these things.

IF ANGELS AND DEMONS EXIST, WHERE ARE THEY?

Some progressives find it hard to accept that Old Testament accounts of angels and "sons of God" are proof for the existence of supernatural beings, preferring to relegate the stories to tribal folklore. The problem for skeptical Christians, who otherwise believe the good news of Christ, lies in the Gospels themselves. If Jesus was wrong about the existence of angels and demons, about whom He frequently spoke, it would be hard to take Him seriously about anything else.

If supernatural beings—angels and demons—truly exist, they must be *somewhere*. Since humans are confined to a three-dimensional world, might we not assume that other self-willed beings created by the same God would have similar constraints? If biblical accounts are true that angels and demons frequently pop in and out of human reality, how do they do it? Why are they allowed to transgress realms where they ought to be confined? Are they free to roam the earth at will? Where do they come from? How do they get back? Why can we not see them?

A better question is this: How is it that some people *can* see them, or at least have claimed to have seen and interacted with angels and demons? Should these people be believed or dismissed as having overactive imaginations subject to the power of suggestion and hallucination? Before proposing a theory for how such things might be, let me first be clear that I myself have never seen an angel or a demon. Nevertheless, I believe they exist because the Bible says they do and because I have heard people tell stories of angelic or demonic encounters that defy a natural explanation.

Likewise most of us have never seen a virus or bacterium. Nonetheless, we have complete confidence in the testimony of scientists and medical professionals who not only have seen them but who also have learned in many cases how to combat and contain them. Therefore we have faith in their testimony that what we cannot see is the true cause of illness, which we can see. Why do we accept the existence of something that cannot be observed by human eyes? Because scientists and doctors have access to something most of us do not:

microscopes that enable them to observe that which is invisible to the natural eye.

Many people claim to have experienced visitations from both good and evil surreal entities, often while being in a highly charged spiritual environment such as a revival meeting. I have yet to personally observe the paranormal manifestations often associated with renewal movements of the past thirty years, though I have intentionally put myself in places where such things are said to have happened. I have not seen gold dust drift down on people, gold teeth appear in mouths, or jewels fall from the sky. I have not seen clouds form in the sanctuary, spontaneous healing from incurable diseases, or limbs grow on human bodies. I have heard testimonies of many who say they have seen these extraordinary occurrences, and with few exceptions I tend to accept that what people claim to have seen is, in fact, what they saw.

How can we discern whether reports of supernatural encounters are real or the products of spiritual delirium? Would we believe the person's eyewitness account of anything else? For example, if the same person observed a crime taking place and then identified a suspect, would we accept him or her as a reliable witness? If the answer is yes, then we should accept that what might be foreign to our own experience is indeed possible in someone else's. As it has been said, a person with a testimony is never at the mercy of a person with a theory.

LOCATION, LOCATION, LOCATION

Reports of interaction with angels and demons have been numerous throughout the world, primarily among mystic or spiritual people. If the testimonies are true, why does it seem to happen in some places but not in others? For example, in the 1990s, what led to the revival and ensuing supernatural phenomena in Argentina, and why did it not occur in other parts of South America, where equal missionary fervor and resources also were spent? Why Nigeria, Azusa Street, Toronto, or Brownsville Assembly of God? The explanation might be one of physics as much as one of faith.

Prior generations of Christians did not require proof that heaven, hell, paradise, Satan, angels, and demons existed. There was a willingness to give an inordinate amount of credence to what the Bible said without the need to know how such claims might be possible. The current generation is much less willing to do so primarily because we know so much about the mechanics of the universe in which we live. In only one generation, things once thought to be science fiction or magic have become commonplace.

Some historians have argued that great moves of God can be linked to great innovation in technology. For example, the invention of the printing press coincided with the Reformation, putting the Bible into the hands of ordinary people on a mass scale for the first time in history. Suddenly the claims of religious institutions about what the Bible said could be poked at, challenged, and debated; with one invention the common folk were educated and convinced of the reliability of the Gospels.

The invention of radio and television proved to be major conduits of the spiritual zeal of the fifties and sixties, giving rise to evangelists with mass appeal such as Billy Graham and others. The Internet has done something even grander. Anyone can research anything at any time with a click of a mouse. (Just two decades ago the previous sentence would have made no sense to anyone.)

We live in an amazing time when knowledge is expanding faster than books can be written to contain it. The advance of science and technology into the study of quantum physics is enabling us to understand the complexities and the interconnectivity of what science calls the cosmos but the church calls the spirit world.

WHERE IS HEAVEN?

Heaven is simply not where we thought it was. The journeys of *Voyager* and the Hubble spacecraft have shown us immense expanses of space where paradise is supposed to be but apparently is not. Bill Bryson, author of *A Short History of Nearly Everything*, explains that it is so difficult for us to imagine how far we have looked into the vastness of the universe because our perceptions of the cosmos have often been based on charts and maps from elementary school.

> On a design of the solar system to scale, with the earth reduced to about the diameter of a pea, Jupiter would be over a thousand feet away and Pluto would be a mile and half distant (and about the size of a bacterium, so you wouldn't be able to see it anyway). On the same scale, Proxima Centauri, our nearest star, would be almost ten thousand miles away. Even if you shrank down everything so that Jupiter was as small as the period at the end of this sentence, and Pluto was no bigger than a molecule, Pluto would still be over thirty-five feet away.
>
> Pluto may be the last object marked on schoolroom

charts, but the system doesn't end there. In fact it isn't even close to ending there. We won't get to the solar system's edge until we have passed through the Oort cloud, a vast celestial realm of drifting comets, and we won't reach the Oort cloud for another ten thousand years.

Based on what we know now and can reasonably imagine, there is absolutely no prospect that any human being will ever visit the edge of our own solar system.[14]

Without entering the debate as to whether heaven and paradise are the same thing, Bryson's conclusion creates a real problem for those who tend toward a literal interpretation of the New Testament. Jesus said He was going "today" to paradise (Luke 23:43), a place the apostle Paul said he knew a "man in Christ" also to go (2 Cor. 12:2–4). Moses and Elijah returned from the place of the righteous dead and made a visitation to Jesus in view of three of His disciples in Matthew 17:3. If these stories are true, wherever paradise might be, it would have to be closer to the planet than the twenty-five thousand years it would take for a human to travel from the edge of the solar system (where telescopes have seen and heaven is not) to earth.

It does not work to say these men in Scripture traveled in spirit and therefore physics do not apply. Jesus left and returned in the same body He was crucified in. The man Paul refers to was the same person before and after he returned from paradise. When Moses and Elijah appeared with Jesus, they seemed to be as human as He was. Unless it is somewhere close by, many things the Bible says about heaven would be impossible.

- God hears us from heaven (2 Chron. 6, et al.).

- God sent bread from heaven (Neh. 9).

- Fire fell from heaven (Job 1, et al.).

- Heaven has pillars (Job 26).

- God looks down from heaven (Ps. 14).

- There are boundaries in heaven (Ps. 19).

- God sends help from heaven (Ps. 57, et al.).

- There are doors in heaven (Ps. 78).

- There is treasure in heaven (Luke 18).

- Signs come from heaven (Luke 21).

- Sound comes from heaven (Acts 2).

- Stephen gazed into heaven (Acts 7).

- Peter saw heaven open and a sheet descend (Acts 10).

- Light comes from heaven (Acts 26).

- Heaven has at least three domains (2 Col. 12).

If Moses, Elijah, Jesus, Paul, angels, and demons can transport themselves between the planes of another dimension and earth instantaneously, then heaven must exist in some other location than what we previously thought. How can we understand this? Romans 1:20 tells us that the invisible qualities of God can be known by what is visible. Is it possible that what quantum physics has now made visible to us can reveal something previously unknown about where heaven might be? Bill Bryson writes:

> According to the new theory, an electron moving between orbits would disappear from one and reappear instantaneously in another *without visiting the space in between*. This idea [is] the famous "quantum leap."[15]

> The uncertainty around which the theory is built is that we can know the path an electron takes as it moves through a space or we can know where it is at a given instant, but we cannot know both.[16]

> Perhaps the most arresting of quantum improbabilities is the idea arising from Wolfgang Pauli's Exclusion Principle of 1925, that the subatomic particles in certain pairs, even when separated by the most considerable distance, can each instantly "know" what the other is doing. Particles have a quality known as spin and, according to quantum theory, the moment you determine the spin of one particle, its sister particle, no matter how distant away, will immediately begin spinning in the opposite direction and at the same rate.[17]

If an electron can instantly move through multiple dimensions of reality without being encumbered by the space between, is it so far-fetched to suppose that there may be another realm, populated by intelligent beings of a different physical makeup than humans, who can move about according to the same physics as an electron? Suppose that these entities are generally confined to a plane of reality parallel to our own and very close by—but sometimes they are able to pass through from one dimension to another.

THIN PLACES

The idea of a veil separating the manifest presence of God from the sight of human beings is well documented in Scripture:

> When Moses finished speaking to them, he put a veil over his face. But whenever he entered the LORD's presence to speak with him, he removed the veil until he came out. And when he came out and told the Israelites what he had been commanded, they saw that his face was radiant. Then Moses would put the veil back over his face until he went in to speak with the LORD.
>
> —EXODUS 34:33–35

> Thick clouds veil him, so he does not see us as he goes about in the vaulted heavens.
>
> —JOB 22:14

> But whenever anyone turns to the Lord, the veil is taken away.
>
> —2 CORINTHIANS 3:16

Perhaps it would be easier for us to grasp the idea of a parallel universe if we consider that it is already part of our earthly experience. We live on dry land at the edge of another world: the sea. It has been said that science knows more about the surface of the moon than what is hidden in the depths of the oceans. God told Job that He had created the sea with fixed limits, doors, and bars in place and commanded it, "This far you may come and no farther; here is where your proud waves halt" (Job 38:11).

And yet we know there are times when the seas breach their boundaries and spill their fury onto the dry land in natural phenomena such as tsunamis. What if there exists another universe as near to us as the sea to the dry land? Suppose this plane of being is as invisible to us as the electron to the naked eye but no less real. Between that world and ours there is a spiritual veil that limits movement for the inhabitants of both.

In the Gospel of Luke Abraham said to the rich man concerning the dead Lazarus, "Between us and you a great chasm has been fixed, so that those who want to go from here to you cannot, nor can anyone cross over from there to us" (Luke 16:26).

Now suppose there are places between these two worlds where the veil is very thin. So thin that gold dust can be blown through it. So thin that "a great cloud of witnesses" can see through it. So thin that those long dead can step through it: Samuel, Moses, Elijah, Jesus, and sometimes, angels and demons. And Satan.

"Where have you been?" God said to Satan.

"Going to and fro across the earth."

I have often been perplexed when Christians fear the advance of science and technology, as if discovering how God gets things done threatens His sovereignty. He is not somehow diminished if we figure out how He did it; in fact, knowing more about how God strategizes is a necessary requirement if we take seriously the idea of ruling and reigning with Him in this life and the next.

Our imagination should be captivated and our spirits soar when a discovery is made that exposes another component in the vastness and complexity of God's creation. Recently I watched an episode of a multipart documentary *How Time Travel Works* on the Discovery Channel (also available on HowStuffWorks.com) about wormholes, those mysterious black holes in space where the gravity is so thick it can pull stars into the center where they disappear. Here is the synopsis of an interview between a producer and one of the astrophysicists:

"Where do you think these wormholes lead?" asked the reporter.

"Possibly to another universe," the physicist answered.

"Would it ever be possible for a human to pass through one of them?"

"Perhaps, but he would have to be willing to die in the process."[18]

Between this world and the supernatural world there is a veil. The pathway between the two usually involves death—but perhaps not always.

Chapter 5

THE DAUGHTERS OF MEN

A s WE DISCUSSED in the last chapter, there are portals between astral planes of the current reality akin to the wormholes in space, thin places in the veil that separate dimensions and through which angels and demons pass easily. This is the testimony of Scripture and that of thousands of men and women who claim to have seen and interacted with supernatural visitors. It is commonly believed among

Christians that demons were once angels whose holy nature was corrupted by their disobedience.

Although this may be true, it may not explain the type of deliverance from evil spirits Jesus and others in the New Testament practiced. Demons (fallen angels) and *demonic spirits*, whom Jesus rebuked and disciples are told to cast out, are not the same things. While angels and idol gods (fallen archangels, as Baal may have been) are common in the Old Testament, there is no evidence that they desired to inhabit human bodies. Yet by the time Jesus arrived, demonic invasion of people was common. If not fallen angels, what are the demonic spirits that take refuge in flesh and blood? A more pressing question may be, where do they go when they are cast out?

Matthew 24 presents us with a long and detailed sermon by Jesus about things that were to happen in the future. With the benefit of history we are able to understand that much of what Jesus warned about actually happened between A.D. 66 and 70, culminating in the brutal destruction of Jerusalem under the Romans. Apart from what we can catalog as actual events having already happened, to which there were at least two important historical witnesses, some of what Jesus said is still cloaked in mystery.

There are primarily three theological arguments for what Jesus meant by His warnings to His disciples. In the first argument Jesus was not talking about a second coming to the earth since the disciples did not expect Him to leave and would have had no frame of reference for a return later in history. Rather He was speaking of His coming/returning to heaven.

Another interpretation assigns the celestial phenomena and earthly events contained in Jesus's prophecy to the siege of Jerusalem as recorded in the eyewitness accounts of Josephus, a Jewish historian, and Tacitus, a Roman historian, who observed and wrote about what they saw in the heavens over Jerusalem between the death of Nero and the final conquest and burning of the temple by the Roman armies in 70.

The third and most popular present-day interpretation of what Jesus was talking about was His return to earth at some-time in the future, the time of which neither He nor His angels knew. Let's suppose this is the correct interpretation.

Jesus said there would be signs that would signal His return, including famines, earthquakes, wars, and persecution. Unfortunately, these signs have not proved helpful since they have all been present in every generation before and after Jesus. There was only one distinctive in what Jesus said to look for, an odd marker that while largely lost to Western interpreters of Scripture would have been easily understood by the people who were present. We know this to be the case because no one asked Him what He meant. Jesus said, "As it was in the days of Noah, so it will be at the coming of the Son of Man" (Matt. 24:37).

Verse 38 goes on to describe the oblivion of the people living at His return who would be found to be eating, drinking, and marrying as if nothing unusual were happening. While Jesus may have been making a point about the *laissez-faire* attitude of the culture, there must be something more to what He was telling them. After all, eating, drinking, and marrying are characteristic of everyday life—against which there is no condemnation. That is, unless something extraordinary and evil had become interwoven into the common life of Noah's day. Since Jesus said it would happen again and would be a sign of His return, perhaps we ought to try to figure out what He was talking about. What remarkable thing was going on in the time of Noah?

THE SONS OF GOD AND THE DAUGHTERS OF MEN

> Now it came about, when men began to multiply on the face of the land, and daughters were born to them, that the sons of God saw that the daughters of men were beautiful; and they took wives for themselves, whomever they chose....The Nephilim were on the earth in those days, and also afterward, when the sons of God came in to the daughters of men, and they bore children to them. Those were the mighty men who were of old, men of renown.
>
> —GENESIS 6:1–4, NAS

Who were the sons of God? This term is translated from the Hebrew *ben 'elohiym*, or "sons of Elohim," which is a term consistently used in the Old Testament for angels. It is never used to mean Jewish people or believers. It was not until after the third century that any attempts were made to translate this term to mean anything other than what it appears to say: angels were attracted to human women, had sex with them, and brought forth a hybrid race known as the Nephilim.

According to the Hebrew lexicon, the term "married any of them they chose" implies an action of a superior power over an inferior partner. In other words, it is to say that the daughters were coerced and did not voluntarily submit to be part of the marriage. When Jesus told His disciples that conditions on the earth at the time of His return would be like the days of Noah when people were given in marriage, the men would have understood Him to be talking about the time in history when the angels forced themselves on human women. With this perspective the meaning of a puzzling statement made by the apostle Paul centuries later becomes understandable.

> For this reason, and because of the angels, the woman ought to have a sign of authority on her head.
> —1 CORINTHIANS 11:10

The belief that angels were attracted to women because of their hair was widespread in the common culture as late as the first century. According to Boyd, "Indeed, during the intertestamental period, we shall later see, this interbreeding of divine beings with human women was often identified as the first fall of the angels. According to this tradition, these 'sons of God' were angels who were charged with caring for humans (they were sometimes called 'the Watchers'). But like the god of Persia in Daniel 10, they forsook their duties and abused their divine authority. Their progeny were thus giant, hybrid, evil beings who furthered the corruption of the earth."[1]

In the fifth century the idea of angels having intimate relations with women became a great embarrassment to the church fathers. Specifically, Celsus and Julian the Apostate used the traditional angel interpretation to attack Christianity. Julius Africanus as well as Cyril of Alexandria and Augustine resorted to another translation in order to ward off the attacks. Angelology, along with other supernatural aspects of the faith, was becoming an embarrassment to the young church as it struggled with legitimacy.[2]

THE SETHITE VIEW

Before moving forward in our quest to understand how angels and demons have interacted with humanity historically and what it may mean to us now, let us first look at the alternative explanation for an interpretation of Genesis 6 offered hundreds of years later by the concerned church fathers.

> Adam had relations with his wife again; and she gave birth to a son, and named him Seth, for, she said, "God has appointed me another offspring in place of Abel, for Cain killed him." To Seth, to him also a son was born; and he called his name Enosh. Then men began to call upon the name of the LORD.
>
> —GENESIS 4:25–26, NAS

There is little debate as to the reason God caused a flood that wiped out all living things—to rid the earth of the Nephilim. The argument is over who the Nephilim were. The alternative view to the offspring of angels is the more modern interpretation that Nephilim were the offspring of Cain whom the earth must be rid of so that the lines of righteous Seth, including Noah, could be saved.

While this explanation may have satisfied the angst of some church fathers who were desperate for an alternative interpretation to the idea of sex between humans and angels, it simply does not match what the earliest Old Testament writings say or how they were interpreted for thousands of years. Further, there is no evidence in Scripture that the line of Seth was godly. No one beyond Noah's immediate family was given protection from the flood. If the lines of Seth were so faithful, why did they perish in the Flood along with all other living things?

What about Seth's son Enosh, often lauded as a man who worshipped Yahweh? There is textual evidence that, rather than a reputation for piety because he "began to call upon the name of the LORD," he may have initiated the practice of profaning the name of God. The words for the action of Enosh are *chalal* ("began"), which means "to profane," and *qara'* ("to call"), which is the idea of accosting a person, to call out.

WHO WERE THE NEPHILIM?

The word *Nephilim* is Hebrew, and in some translations it reads "giants." "Heroes," used by the NIV in Genesis 6:4, is an unfortunate translation. In the King James Version it reads "mighty." In fact, it is a very difficult word to translate into English, and in some versions of the Bible it is not attempted. But one of the possible translations would be "bloodthirsty." There is a general consensus by scholars on both sides of the Sethite view and the angel view that it was the offspring of "the sons of God" and "the daughters of men" who are cited as the main reason for the Flood. Let's consider that the Sethite view is correct and the Nephilim were the descendants of Cain. What could Cain's line have done to produce progeny that were such an abomination to Yahweh that He wiped out every living thing from the face of the earth?

Procreation by parents of differing religious views does not produce unnatural offspring. The marrying of unbelievers and believers does not produce abnormal creatures. One interesting note is the Nephilim appear to be only men. There is no mention of women in the narrative, though it is common in this line of Scripture to mention both men and women when both are involved. The most dramatic testimony as to who the Nephilim might have been is found in God's response to their effect on the earth.

> The LORD said, "I will blot out man whom I have cre-
> ated from the face of the land, from man to animals to
> creeping things and to birds of the sky; for I am sorry
> that I have made them."
>
> —GENESIS 6:7, NAS

Whatever provoked God to such action was outside the scope of the sin we know about from other scriptures. Old Testament accounts tell us how God responded to murder, theft, idol worship, lying, licentiousness, child sacrifice, sexual sin, and many others. But we do not see Him destroy the entire population of humanity and animals as a remedy. The severity of His retort meant something had gone desperately wrong with the world, the cause of which had to be eradicated along with the creation itself. But why *everything*?

If the Sethite view is correct, then the Nephilim were nothing more than the reprobate sons of Cain who committed aggressive sexual sin against attractive women. Reprehensible as it may have been, the rape of women by invading tribes was a common consequence of war. A more puzzling question would be, what does a human atrocity have to do with the corruption of the entire scope of the animal kingdom? Archeology provides evidence of a widespread belief that the sin of the marauding angels went far beyond the seduction and/or rape of human women.

They Left a Note

The mythology of many ancient cultures can be found in art-work and etchings on caves and rocks in many countries spanning a large part of the world. Throughout the centuries crude wall drawings evolved into sophisticated paintings and sculptures, some of which are displayed in museums today. Many of the artists' renditions depict a common theme of creatures that appear to be half-animal and half-human, or half-animal and half-angel, such as the winged horse. The myth is so common that it survives even today in children's fairy tales. An example of the universality of this idea can be found in the chronicles of an Egyptian historian named Manethos, who wrote extensively about half-human, half-animal creatures and credits the gods with their creation.

> And they [the gods] were said to have brought forth double-winged human beings, also others with four wings and two faces; and with one body and two heads, man and woman, male and female within one creature; still other human beings had thighs of goats and horns upon their heads; others had the feet of horses; others were horses behind and men in front; there were also said to have been man-headed bulls and four-bodied dogs, whose tails emerged like fish-tails from their backs; also horses with heads of dogs...and other monsters, such as all kinds of dragon-like beings...and a great number of wondrous creatures, variously formed and all different from one another, whose images they ranged one beside the other in the Temple of Belos, and preserved.[3]

Why did God destroy every living thing to rid the world of the Nephilim? It can only be that the gene pools of animals and humans were corrupted beyond rehabilitation.

THE NEPHILIM AFTER THE FLOOD

The heading above is distressing. If the purpose of the Flood was to destroy the Nephilim and start over with a cleansed gene pool, it does not seem to have worked. The Book of Numbers reports how Moses selected a dozen men, including Caleb and Joshua, to spy out the land the wandering Israelites were about to enter. The men returned to tell him and Aaron that the land was indeed fruitful and rich, but there was a problem with the inhabitants.

> The land through which we have gone, in spying it out, is a land that devours its inhabitants; and all the people whom we saw in it are men of great size. There also we saw the Nephilim (the sons of Anak are part of the Nephilim); and we became like grasshoppers in our own sight, and so we were in their sight.
>
> —NUMBERS 13:32–33, NAS

How could this happen? Centuries after Noah's flood we find the Promised Land again filled with the dreaded Nephilim. How did they get there—particularly if they were only male, which means they could not breed? How could they have survived the centuries between Noah and Moses? A woefully inadequate answer is that angels are eternal and do not die. The Nephilim were only partly angelic; the human part of their being would have been subject to death and decay.

What happened to their angelic nature when their human hosts died, as is the fate of all flesh?

From the time of Noah to the time of Joshua, did the eternal spirits of the Nephilim pass through the generations, invading new humans along the way? If this happened, when did it cease to happen? Could this explain what the demon spirits in the New Testament actually were and why we see them attempting to reinhabit humans?

Our conundrum is our steadfast insistence that God's plans do not fail and therefore all the Nephilim who were present during Noah's day were killed. If this is so, how do we account for their presence centuries later? Jewish folklore tells of how Og, mentioned many times in the Old Testament as the Nephilim king, survived the Flood by hiding in the rafters of the ark, where Noah fed him to keep him quiet. Whether true or not, the story does not help us with the presence of the Nephilim on the earth in later times.

If the Flood successfully destroyed all the Nephilim who were alive in Noah's time, it can only be that the violation of human women by rebellious angels continued. The Promised Land the Jews were to conquer was filled with them to the extent that the spies Moses sent out were terrified. More evidence of their presence lies in God's instructions to the Israelites as to what they were to do to the tribes living in the land. They were to destroy them without mercy.

> When the LORD your God brings you into the land where you are entering to possess it, and clears away many nations before you, the Hittites and the Girgashites and the Amorites and the Canaanites and

the Perizzites and the Hivites and the Jebusites, seven nations greater and stronger than you, and when the Lord your God delivers them before you and you defeat them, then you shall utterly destroy them. You shall make no covenant with them and show no favor to them.

Furthermore, you shall not intermarry with them; you shall not give your daughters to their sons, nor shall you take their daughters for your sons. For they will turn your sons away from following Me to serve other gods; then the anger of the Lord will be kindled against you and He will quickly destroy you. But thus you shall do to them: you shall tear down their altars, and smash their sacred pillars, and hew down their Asherim, and burn their graven images with fire.... You shall consume all the peoples whom the Lord your God will deliver to you; your eye shall not pity them, nor shall you serve their gods, for that would be a snare to you.

—Deuteronomy 7:1–5, 16, nas

These verses are so unsettling to modern Christian apologists that many, such as Bishop Shelby Spong, contend that the God of the Old Testament and the God of the New cannot possibly be the same God. Yahweh's merciless orders make it seem likely that the original inhabitants of the Promised Land had fallen into the worship of the fallen angels whom He had originally set as their protectors. But why was there no offer for repentance, no attempt at spiritual rehabilitation of any kind? If God is impartial as Scripture declares, why did He demand such brutality against a native people regardless of their pagan beliefs? His behavior toward them was not consistent with the God of forty years before, who showed Himself patient with the Egyptians, giving them time to believe and allowing thousands of them to leave Egypt along with the Israelites. Why was there no mercy or pity to the people of this land?

One argument holds that the tribes God told Moses to destroy could not be redeemed because their humanity had been corrupted. If correct, it provides evidence that the molestation of human women by rebellious angels happened more than one time in history. If the Nephilim, product of an unholy union between angels and humans, is anything more than folklore, there must be something in the New Testament that supports the legend.

WHAT DOES THE NEW TESTAMENT REVEAL?

In 2 Peter 2 we find the apostle exhorting the new believers to be on guard against false prophets and apostles who would distort the true gospel. In verse 3 he talks about the certainty of judgment upon those who lead the people astray by their deception. It is verses 4 and 5 where things begin to get interesting.

> For if God did not spare angels when they sinned, but sent them to hell, putting them into gloomy dungeons to be held for judgment; if he did not spare the ancient world when he brought the flood on its ungodly people, but protected Noah, a preacher of righteousness, and seven others...
>
> —2 PETER 2:4–5

What is Peter talking about when he refers to the angels who sinned? Some may contend that he meant the angels who rebelled and were cast out of heaven with Lucifer. This is unlikely because Peter did not have access to this information. The Revelation of John had not yet been written, and there are no Old Testament writings that testify to the casting down of Lucifer with one-third of the angelic realm. Our only information about this event comes from Revelation 12:9.

Further, Peter tells the people the period of history he is talking about—the time of Noah. The fact that Peter did not find it necessary to be specific as to what the sin of the angels was is indicative that the details of the story were well known among the people. Jewish people of the first century would have knowledge about the Nephilim not only from their oral history and from the Genesis account but also from ancient writings that are not included in the canonized Old Testament books, such as the Book of Enoch, fragments of which were found in the Dead Sea Scrolls. A passage from the Book of Enoch reads:

> And all the others together with them took unto themselves wives, and each chose for himself one, and they began to go into them and to defile themselves with them, and they taught them charms and enchantments, and the cutting of roots, and made them acquainted with plants. And they became pregnant, and they bare great giants, whose height was three thousand ells: who consumed all the acquisitions of men. And when men could no longer sustain them, the giants turned against them and devoured mankind. And they began to sin against birds, and beasts, and reptiles, and fish,

and to devour one another's flesh and drink the blood.
The earth laid accusation against the lawless ones.[4]

The Greek word Peter used for *hell* in 2 Peter 2:4 is *tartaroo*, or *Tartarus*; it is the only place in the Bible where this term is used. It means "dark abode of woe" and "the pit of darkness in the unseen world." Homer used the word in *The Iliad* as the place of punishment that was "as far beneath Hades as heaven is high above the earth."[5]

The belief in copulation between angels and humans was widely believed in Jesus's time. We will take a look at how this belief impacted His life and the subsequent writings of Paul in more detail in chapter 6. In the meantime, according to the biblical standard of two or three witnesses, is there any place else in the New Testament that alludes to the sin of the angels?

WHAT IS ROMANS 1 ABOUT?

People whose experience does not include being trained to be critical thinkers in response to biblical scholarship tend to give an inordinate amount of credence to commentary, sometimes equating it with Scripture itself. Most do not compare multiple translations of the Bible and, therefore, are not aware of the differences in interpretation from one version to the next. Fewer yet are aware of the multiple sources of commentary and how they differ in explaining how the verses should be understood. Neither does the typical nonacademic consider that the writers of commentary—all of them—are writing from a point of view that reflects the religious discipline in which they were educated. That is why commentaries on chapters such as Matthew 13 can vary widely depending on whether one is writing from a Jewish paradigm or from a Westernized model.

Most often whatever people are told from the pulpit or at a conference about the meaning of Bible verses is pretty much what they believe without questioning whether there might be other legitimate interpretations. Romans 1 is an example of Scripture where the following questions should be asked: Who is Paul speaking to? And what is he talking about? These verses represent a scathing chastisement by Paul, about which there has been little challenge among believers as to whether we have understood it correctly.

> For since the creation of the world God's invisible qualities—his eternal power and divine nature—have been clearly seen, being understood from what has been made, so men are without excuse. For although they knew God, they neither glorified him as God nor gave thanks to him, but their thinking became futile and their foolish hearts were darkened. Although they claimed to be wise, they became fools and exchanged the glory of the immortal God for images made to look like mortal man and birds and animals and reptiles.
>
> Therefore God gave them over in the sinful desires of their hearts to sexual impurity for the degrading of their bodies with one another. They exchanged the truth about God for a lie, and worshiped and served created things rather than the Creator—who is forever praised. Amen.
>
> Because of this, God gave them over to shameful lusts. Even their women exchanged natural sexual relations for unnatural ones. In the same way the men

also abandoned natural relations with women and were inflamed with lust for one another. Men committed shameful acts with other men, and received in themselves the due penalty for their perversion.

Furthermore, since they did not think it worthwhile to retain the knowledge of God, he gave them over to a depraved mind, to do what ought not to be done. They have become filled with every kind of wickedness, evil, greed and depravity. They are full of envy, murder, strife, deceit and malice. They are gossips, slanderers, God-haters, insolent, arrogant and boastful; they invent ways of doing evil; they disobey their parents; they are senseless, faithless, heartless, ruthless. Although they know God's righteous decree that those who do such things deserve death, they not only continue to do these very things but also approve of those who practice them.

—ROMANS 1:20–32

In attempting to understand these verses correctly, it is helpful to remember that Paul did not base his writings on anything Jesus was known to have said as noted by Franciscan monk Richard Rohr: "The letters Paul wrote precede the four Gospels by at least twenty years. When Paul was writing, Mathew, Mark, Luke, and John had not yet been written. And by the time the Gospels appeared, we already had Paul's letters to the Romans, Galatians, Corinthians (first and second), Philemon, and Philippians. This is why Paul never quotes the Gospels."[6]

Jesus did not use descriptors with the same vitriolic rhetoric as Paul in expressing the moral condition of the people of His day. His rebuke was against social injustice, the failure of religious leaders, and the corruption of the temple worship system. Bible scholar N. T. Wright states, "Jesus called people to a simple gospel of repentance, belief and the practice of the Sermon on the Mount; Paul developed a complex theology of justification by faith, something Jesus never mentioned, with all kinds of hard and gritty bits quite alien to the original message."[7]

Jesus simply did not lambaste the ordinary citizens with the hateful accusations of Romans 1, nor does Paul anywhere else in his epistles. So why such a wrathful commentary in this chapter? Perhaps it was because Paul was not criticizing the people of his generation as is popularly believed. He was talking about something else.

Verse 20 reveals that Paul is talking about "men" who have been around since the creation of the world who would have clearly understood the divine nature of God without impediment, such that they are without excuse for their behavior. Does that accurately portray the history of mankind? No, if for no other reason than mankind has not been around since the creation of the world.

Verse 22–23 accuse whomever Paul is talking about of claiming to be wise but becoming as fools and exchanging the glory of the immortal God for images made to look like mortal human beings and birds and animals and reptiles. These verses bear an odd resemblance to Genesis 6:7, where God was speaking about the coming flood and said He would blot them out along with the animals, the birds, and the creatures that move along the ground.

Verses 24–26 of Romans 1 tell us that God gave whomever Paul is talking about "over in the sinful desires of their hearts to sexual impurity for the degrading of their bodies with one another." They exchanged the truth about God for a lie and worshipped and served created things rather than the Creator; because of this, God gave them over to shameful lusts where even their women exchanged natural sexual relations for unnatural ones.

Was this really the condition of the Jewish population in the first century? If so, why did Jesus not comment on what would have been an extraordinary breakdown in the moral condition of the people? Why did not Matthew, Luke, John, James, or anyone else bother to mention what would have amounted to a complete breakdown in society?

In the New Testament it was commonplace for the author to interlace his contemporary writing with some part of Jewish history to make a point. The writer rarely quoted the source of his analogy because the people knew their history so well it was unnecessary to give a citation. Peter did this in his address on the Day of Pentecost by quoting long passages from Joel and Psalms. Paul followed the practice as well in 1 Corinthians 1:19; 2:9; 2 Corinthians 6:2; Galatians 4:27; and in many other places.

It seems worth considering that what Paul was describing in Romans 1 had nothing to do with the moral condition of the people of the first century or centuries to come. He was referring to the time before Noah's flood when the angels rebelled and brought about the desecration of themselves and humans in such a way that God "gave them over to their shameful lusts" so that the gene pool of humans and animals had to be destroyed.

THE STRANGE EXHORTATION OF JUDE

Jude shared concerns similar to those of Peter about false teachers infiltrating the young church and leading the people astray. He described them this way:

> For certain persons have crept in unnoticed, those who were long beforehand marked out for this condemnation, ungodly persons who turn the grace of our God into licentiousness and deny our only Master and Lord, Jesus Christ.
>
> —JUDE 4, NAS

Jude then becomes as passionate as Peter in declaring what the fate of such men would be like.

> And angels who did not keep their own domain, but abandoned their proper abode, He has kept in eternal bonds under darkness for the judgment of the great day.
>
> —JUDE 6, NAS

The word Jude uses for "own domain" is *arche*, which means as something was in the beginning or as it was created to be. The word for "abode" is *oiketerion*, which means housing or, in this case, bodies. In other words, Jude is describing an action by the angels that caused them to violate the limits of their naturally created state and now await a day of utter darkness for their actions. Again, the lack of detail as to what the sin was indicates that the story was widely known and additional attribution was unnecessary.

But there is more to this epistle. Frankly, I have seriously considered not including the following possible interpretation of Jude 7 in this book. The religious wrath and political controversy it is sure to stir up among some Christians is almost certain. But to ignore a legitimate speculation about cosmic evil (which, if correct, may have severely warped our application of Scripture) only for the purpose of avoiding criticism and religious ire seems to me to be intellectually dishonest. Having said that, let the reader beware.

THE REAL SIN OF SODOM AND GOMORRAH

> Just as Sodom and Gomorrah and the cities around them, since they in the same way as these indulged in gross immorality and went after strange flesh, are exhibited as an example in undergoing the punishment of eternal fire.
>
> —JUDE 7, NAS

We cannot interpret Jude's writing without the framework of what Genesis tells us happened in Sodom and Gomorrah.

> Now the two angels came to Sodom in the evening as Lot was sitting in the gate of Sodom. When Lot saw them, he rose to meet them and bowed down with his face to the ground. And he said, "Now behold, my lords, please turn aside into your servant's house, and spend the night, and wash your feet; then you may rise early and go on your way." They said however, "No, but we shall spend the night in the square." Yet he urged them strongly, so they turned aside to him and entered his house; and he prepared a feast for them, and baked unleavened bread, and they ate. Before they lay down, the men of the city, the men of Sodom, surrounded the house, both young and old,

all the people from every quarter; and they called to Lot and said to him, "Where are the men who came to you tonight? Bring them out to us that we may have relations with them."

—Genesis 19:1–5, nas

The word used for "relations" in verse 5 is one of the most hotly contested words in Scripture. Here are all the possible translations and number of uses:

3045, *yada*, a primitive root, to know: ability (1), acknowledge (4), acknowledged (2), acquaintances (5), acquainted (1), aware (6), becomes known (1), bring forth (1), cared (1), chosen (2), clearly understand (2), cohabit (1), comprehend (1), concern (2), concerned (1), consider (3), declare (1), detected (1), directed (1), discern (2), disciplined (1), discovered (3), distinguish (1), endowed (3), experienced (4), experiences (1), familiar friend (1), find (5), found (1), gain (1), had knowledge (1), had relations (6), had...relations (1), has (1), has regard (1), has...knowledge (1), have (4), have relations (3), have...knowledge (2), ignorant (1), illiterate (1), indeed learn (1), inform (1), informed (4), instruct (3), instructed (1), intimate friends (1), investigate (2), knew (38), know (542), know for certain (4), know with certainty (1), know assuredly (1), know well (1), knowing (5), knowledge (4), known (65), knows (54), knows well (1), lain (1), leading (1), learn (7), learned (1), literate (1), made himself known (2), made it known (1), made myself known (2), made known (10), make himself known (1), make his known (1), make it known (1), make my known (1), make myself known (4), make them known (1), make your known (1), make yourself known (1), make known (14), notice (2), observe (2), perceive (1), perceived (1), possibly know (1), predict (1), professional mourners (1), provided (1), raped (1), read (1), realize (1), realized (5), recognize (2), recognized (1), regard (1), satisfied (1), seems (1), show (3), shown (1), skillful (3), sure (1), take knowledge (1), take note (1), take notice (1), taught (2), teach (6), tell (3), tells (1), took notice (1), unaware (1), unawares (1), understand (10), understands (1), understood (3), unknown (1), very well know (1), well aware (1)[8]

The most respected of biblical commentators are unable to agree on how this word should be translated. Below are two additional examples from the New International Version and the King James Version.

> They called to Lot, "Where are the men who came to you tonight? Bring them out to us so that *we can have sex with them*."
>
> —GENESIS 19:5, EMPHASIS ADDED

> And they called unto Lot, and said unto him, Where are the men which came in to thee this night? Bring them out unto us, that *we may know them*.
>
> —GENESIS 19:5, KJV, EMPHASIS ADDED

As fiercely contested as the correct translation may be, it is generally taught in evangelicalism that this verse refers to homosexuality. Setting aside all presupposition, what does the narrative tell us is going on?

All translations agree that two angels came to visit Lot,

Abraham's nephew, in Sodom. The men of the city demanded the visitors come outside and referred to them as *men*. When Lot saw them, he greeted them as *lords*. There are other passages of Scripture where angels are identified as appearing as men. This may mean that while Lot and his neighbors saw the same people, they used different words meaning the same thing to identify them.

Now let us suppose that conventional wisdom is correct and verse 5 does indeed mean the men of Sodom wanted to have sex with the visitors. The key question becomes, did they want to have sex with them because they were *men* or because they were *angels*? Jude 7 tells us that the gross immorality of Sodom and Gomorrah was "going after strange flesh" (KJV). What does this term mean? According to Strong's Hebrew/Greek dictionary, here are the actual words and their possible translations:

- "strange," *heteros*; of uncertain orgin, "other": another (31), another one (2), any other (1), different (6), else (2), one (1), other (31), strange (1), strangers (1)[9]

- "flesh," *sarx*; a primitive word, "flesh": bodily (2), bodily condition (1), body (2)[10]

The term "strange flesh" is not used anywhere in the Bible as a reference to homosexuality. Based on what Scripture actually says, not on commentary, the argument must be made that the perversion of Sodom and Gomorrah had nothing to do with homosexuality and everything to do with the desire to have sexual relations with angels.

WHAT DID JESUS MEAN?

As it was in the days of Noah, so it will be at the coming of the Son of Man.

—MATTHEW 24:37

There is an important clue in the writings of the prophet Daniel that may help us correctly understand what Paul was talking about in Romans 1 and what Jesus meant in Matthew 24:37. In describing a vision of the end of the age—again, we will not debate here whether Daniel is viewing the end of the age of temple worship A.D. 70 or the end of the modern age in which we are living—Daniel saw a strange statue representing the various kingdoms that were to come. In describing the last age he used these words:

And in that you saw the iron mixed with common clay, they will combine with one another in the seed of men; but they will not adhere to one another, even as iron does not combine with pottery.

—DANIEL 2:43, NAS

Daniel testifies that near the end of the age something unnatural will attempt to combine with the seed of humanity. Jesus said something identifiable with the days of Noah would be widespread at the coming of the Son of Man. Whatever bias we as modern rationalists may have against such a notion, the common denominator in the biblical narrative is angels who penetrated the veil between heaven and earth for the purpose of sexual relations with humans. If this is true, when did it cease to happen? Or has it?

MODERN ENCOUNTERS OF THE THIRD KIND

As Bible teacher Chuck Missler and others have postulated, there is a growing concern within the psychiatric community from the strange and far too frequent reports from people who claim to have been abducted by UFOs. The reports are too bizarre to accept and yet too frequent and consistent to ignore. While we may be tempted to dismiss these reports as untrustworthy, sensational, and the fodder of tabloids, what the Bible refers to as *angels*, in which we do believe, and what modern society refers to as *aliens*, about which we are not sure what to believe, may be different terms for a similar phenomena.

The late John E. Mack—a professor of psychiatry at the Cambridge Hospital at Harvard Medical School, a Pulitzer Prize winner, and an author of more than 150 peer-reviewed papers in medical journals—shocked the professional community by stating that he believed the abduction reports are real. Further, from the interviews he conducted with the abductees, he said that he believed the aliens appeared to have an agenda to develop a hybrid race.[11]

At a professional conference on abductions at MIT, Dr. Mack asked the provocative question, "If what these abductees are saying is happening to them *isn't* happening, what *is*?"[12]

Chapter 6

JESUS—SON OF AN ANGEL?

IN JESUS'S TIME a young man who exhibited an extraordinary grasp of the holy writings, as Jesus did, would have been whisked by the Pharisees into training at an early age to become a rabbi. It can be safely assumed that Jesus was not chosen in part because of the unresolved issue of who His father was. Joseph, by his own admission, was not His father, which Mary confirmed. The unsettled issue of paternity in early Jewish culture was sure to have dogged Jesus as a child and young man. Psalm 69 is believed by many to be a prophetic lament about the scorn Jesus endured as an illegitimate child:

For I endure scorn for your sake,
    and shame covers my face.
I am a stranger to my brothers,
    an alien to my own mother's sons;
for zeal for your house consumes me,
    and the insults of those who insult you fall on me.
When I weep and fast,
    I must endure scorn;
when I put on sackcloth,
    people make sport of me.
Those who sit at the gate mock me,
    and I am the song of the drunkards.
—Psalm 69:7–12, emphasis added

After Jesus was baptized by John the Baptist and returned from His encounter with Satan in the desert, multitudes began to follow Him. Because of the miracles throngs were anxious to believe Jesus was the long-expected Messiah. Few, however, were willing to believe He was also the begotten Son of God. Many others, based on the testimonies of Mary, Joseph, and the shepherds, suspected He might be the son of an angel.

A challenge for modern readers of the New Testament is to keep in mind that it was penned by and to a people with a long religious history that represented a worldview significantly different from the Westernized interpretation held by most evangelicals today. The New Testament writings have survived the passage of centuries with minimal change, as no other writing of antiquity is known to have done. However, while the words may not have changed significantly over time, some of the meanings have.

For example, in 1 Peter 3:6 the King James Version uses the word *amazement* to express the feeling of terror or fear. And instead of using the phrase "by and by," as the KJV does several times in the Gospels (Matt. 13:21; Mark 6:25; Luke 17:7; 21:9), we would not say "immediately"—a very different meaning indeed. When the Bible mentions an apple or blackberry, it does not mean a computer or cell phone, which would be the common interpretation of such words today. Rationalist thought has changed how moderns understand the meaning, particularly concerning the supernatural.

In the corporate memory of first-century people, the ancient belief that humans were at times the objects of sexual aggression by angels resulting in offspring was a filter through which any new reports about angelic encounters must pass. From the Gospel writings, the accounts of angelic visitations by Mary and Joseph resulting in an unusual pregnancy were not refuted or rejected as fantasy by the hearers, as would certainly be the case if such an event happened today. Yet the only ones who found the claim remarkable enough to investigate came two years later when a troop of oriental monarchs and astrologers went in search of Mary and Joseph.

At the time of Jesus all nations of antiquity, including the Jews, Romans, and Greeks, believed in a multiplicity of "gods" that frequently interacted with humanity. Therefore a report of the appearance of a host of angels to a group of shepherds in a field might not have been as remarkable to them as it would be to us. The fact that modern Christians by huge margins continue to believe the accounts as brought forth in

Matthew and Luke speaks more to the current faith than to the ancient one. After all this time, why do educated, modern people still believe the circumstances surrounding Jesus's birth pretty much as told in the Gospels? Some scholars have remarked that the most persuasive argument for confidence in the authenticity of the third Gospel is because of who wrote it.

Luke was not "of the circumcision"; therefore he was not a Jew. He was a physician and the most cultured of the New Testament writers. He was disciplined in his writing and a stickler for facts. As an example, some academics believe Luke wrote the Book of Acts as a legal brief to present before Rome on Paul's behalf. Acts terminates abruptly because Paul was either executed or released unexpectedly. It is unlikely that Dr. Luke would have been party to writing the sensational account of Jesus's birth unless he was convinced that the testimony of the witnesses was true. The first-century audience for Luke's writings did not demand that he produce evidence for the amazing accounts he wrote about because the people were well acquainted with the amazing. Their history was replete with reports of angels interrupting the natural affairs of mankind.

An analogy as to how ancient people understood the supernatural is to think about the present world in which we live and our relationship with technology. It is part of our common vernacular to refer to the Internet or the blogosphere as if it were an ethereal dimension, of which few of us understand the mechanics but all of us access on a daily basis. We tap into this world on computers that do not plug into anything. We are a wireless society moving between the natural world of matter into a seemingly unlimited, invisible world of digital information that we can download and print out with ease.

Most of us cannot begin to explain how this happens, but none of us doubt that it does. Fewer than two decades ago most of what we take today as commonplace technology would have been considered the stuff of science fiction. Therefore, today when we talk about what we read, heard, or saw on the Internet, we do not have to offer proof of the science behind our statements. Even in third world countries where many cannot read or write, the belief in a digital world that cannot be seen or explained is common to the general population.

DID MARY AND JOSEPH TELL THE TRUTH?

Mary's and Joseph's claims that they were individually visited by an angelic being do not appear to have been in dispute. The chatter was about the suspicious circumstances leading to Mary's pregnancy. Whether she was visited by an angel does not appear to have been argued. But there must have been considerable speculation as to what the nature of the encounter really was.

According to Luke's Gospel the angel Gabriel appeared to a young woman named Mary and told her she would become pregnant by the action of the Holy Spirit. Mary, a girl of about fourteen years of age, must have told her parents, her friends, and Joseph, her fiancé, what had happened. Although they might have been distressed at the news that she was now with child, all of them seemed to have believed her.

There is no scriptural information that Mary's father and mother berated her or accused her of lying, although they did send her away to spend time with her cousin Elizabeth, who was also pregnant through unusual circumstances. Mary's parents believed her because the idea of an angel appearing to a woman who consequently became pregnant was not an unfamiliar one, though it usually ended in something short of a blessed event. Deeply embedded in Jewish consciousness was the Nephilim.

Matthew's Gospel tells us that when Joseph learned of Mary's condition, he decided to put her away secretly, even though it would have been within his rights to publicly accuse her of adultery and have her severely punished, even stoned. It must have been a difficult decision for Joseph to opt for discretion because failing to take action to expunge his honor could have been interpreted to mean he was not as innocent as he claimed to be. Our high-road interpretation of Joseph's response has been that he was gracious to Mary, not wanting to disgrace her for her infidelity.

While this may be true, it would have been an extraordinary act of charity for a man of Joseph's day to behave so generously in the face of incontrovertible evidence of adultery, if that is what he thought had happened. What is more likely to be true is that Joseph believed Mary when she told him about Gabriel's visit. Thinking his betrothed had been accosted by an angel and was pregnant through no fault of her own, he was willing to help her avoid the shame.

Before he could make good on his plan, Joseph himself was visited by an angel who assured him that the child Mary had conceived was of the Holy Spirit—not of a man and not of an angel. Later Joseph would be warned by the same angel to take the child and flee to Egypt to escape Herod's wrath. Soon after the angel's original declaration Joseph took Mary to Bethlehem in keeping with the law requiring a national census be taken. While they were there, the baby was born and the announcement was made by the heavenly host to a group of shepherds.

In a small community like Bethlehem, so near Jerusalem, if these events actually happened, it is almost certain that many other people must have been eyewitnesses to the celestial proclamation of the angels. The Bible does not say that no one else saw what happened, only that the shepherds did. If they had been the only ones to see the heralding angels, the story would most likely have died for lack of a credible witness. Shepherds were simply not considered to be instruments of truth and divine revelation. By the first century the idyllic image of a protector of flocks in the mode of David was long over. Shepherds were generally regarded as untrustworthy bands of gypsies and thieves whose divine encounters were of no interest to anyone.

The Bible comments on the few people who eventually went in search of the child but has nothing to say about those who did not, perhaps because they were simply not important to the story. It must also be remembered that the people who were alive at the time of Jesus did not have access to the detailed accounts of Matthew and Luke, which were not written down until at least fifty years later. Whatever the locals came to know about Jesus, they learned through the grapevine, which carried the news that a local girl named Mary was impregnated by an angel, who subsequently visited Joseph twice to solicit his help in protecting his (the angel's) child.

This speculation is supported by what would later be written in the epistles. Equivalent to an urban myth that will not die, the speculation about Jesus's angelic parentage was so prevalent that both Paul and the writer of Hebrews would vigorously refute the heretical claim that Jesus was the illegitimate child of a Jewish girl and an angel. To the people of that day Jesus, son of an angel, was much more believable than Jesus, Son of God.

THE CONCEPTION OF JESUS IN ISLAM

The heresy did not die with Paul's refutation. Five hundred years later it would appear again in another testament, the Quran.

> She [Mary] said: "O my Lord! how shall I have a son when no man has touched me?" He [the angel] said: "Even so: Allah creates what He wills: when He has decreed a Plan, He but says to it, 'Be,' and it is!"
>
> —SURAH 3:47

> And Mary the daughter of 'Imran, who guarded her chastity; and We breathed into (her body) of Our spirit; and she testified to the truth of the words of her Lord and of His Revelations, and was one of the devout (servants).
>
> —SURAH 66:12

It might surprise Christians to know that Islam honors Jesus as a prophet appointed by God and expects that He will return to earth with Muhammad at the battle of Armageddon. He is not, however, revered as the Son of God. Islam interprets early Christian writings to say that Jesus was born of a virgin who was impregnated by an angel.

Jesus, the son of Mary, had a mother who was truthful, pure, and chosen; chosen by Allah over the women of her age. The Quran has an entire chapter called Maryam (Mary). She was a servant to the temple who was impregnated by a divine angel. Her child testified in the cradle by saying: "I am a servant of Allah. He has given me a book and made me a prophet. He has made be blessed wherever I am."[1]

Then they asked Muhammad who he thought was the father of Jesus. Muhammad remained silent; he had no answer. So Allah sent down a few verses of Sura al Imran (Sura 3) and Sura Maryam (Sura 19)....

In verse 19:17, Allah told Muhammad that an angel (only one angel; contradiction: 3:43, 45 say several angels visited Mary), as a man, appeared to Mary.

According to ibn Kathir, the angel was Gabriel, Allah's soul. He appeared to her complete and perfect in the shape of a man. Gabriel is Allah's Ruh or Soul.

In 19:18, we read that Mary sought protection of Allah from the angel who came to her in the shape of a man. As per ibn Kathir, Mary thought the man (angel) was about to rape her. This means Allah's soul, Gabriel, was menacing. Mary was petrified that this Allah's soul might molest her.

Allah's Soul, archangel Gabriel, informed Mary that Allah is capable of doing anything; her son (Jesus) would be a sign from Allah.

Jalalyn writes that Gabriel breathed into the opening of her shirt, whereupon she sensed the formed foetus in her womb.[2]

Contrary to what many in the modern church may believe, there was no particular expectation among the early Jews that the Messiah would have a supernatural nature. The Western insistence that the Jews believed miracles would accompany the birth of their deliverer appeals to primarily one verse of Scripture.

> Behold, a virgin will be with child and bear a son, and she will call His name Immanuel.
>
> —Isaiah 7:14, nas

Always a subject of debate among theologians, this verse received renewed controversy in April 2011 when the Catholic church agreed with the argument of many language specialists that the Hebrew word *almah* should have been translated as "young woman," not "virgin."[3] The church remains adamant that this announcement should not be viewed as an argument against the belief that Mary was a virgin, only that there was no prerequisite in Jewish thought that the Messiah would be the Son of God or supernaturally unique in any way.

The Angel Controversy in the New Church

The Colossian heresy about which Paul wrote combated philosophical speculations, astral powers, and reverence to angelic intermediaries. From the subjects he touched on Paul was concerned about the inordinate attention still given to the powers of the spirit world to the detriment of the place given to Jesus, particularly concerning angels.

> Let no one keep defrauding you of your prize by delighting in self-abasement and the worship of the angels.
>
> —Colossians 2:18, nas

The writer of Hebrews was equally concerned.

> Having become as much better than the angels, as He has inherited a more excellent name than they. For to which of the angels did He ever say, "You are My Son, today I have begotten You"? And again, "I will be a Father to Him and he shall be a Son to Me"? And when He again brings the firstborn into the world, He says, "And let all the angels of God worship Him."
>
> —HEBREWS 1:4–6, NAS

Paul's concern was that the people did not understand the all-encompassing adequacy of the blood of Jesus for the forgiveness of sin or that Jesus alone was the ultimate arbitrator between themselves and God. Many of those who followed Jesus as the Messiah continued to believe that the hierarchy of angels was still in place, and, therefore, for life to go well, it was still necessary to appease them. In fairness, why would they think anything else? There are twenty-nine mentions of angels in the Gospels, many of them from the mouth of Jesus. Not one of them has anything to say about dismantling the chain of command of governing angels.

ANGELOLOGY AND THE PERSECUTION

Part of the vicious maltreatment of early Christians by Rome was because of a similar theology held by the Romans. Most of us have been taught that the persecution in the early church happened because the believers were loyal to Jesus. This is partially true, but it does not begin to explain why the largest and most efficient military regime in the world involved itself in the affairs of what they considered nothing more than a

Jewish cult. As far as Rome was concerned, the Christians represented nothing other than Jews by a different name.

Roman justice was known worldwide for the impartiality of its court system without regard to regionalized custom or religion. When given a choice between appearing before a Roman court or a Jewish court, Paul chose the former (Acts 25). By the time of Jesus, Rome had conquered many nations with thousands of gods. Once Caesar was added to the cadre of local deities, Rome refused to be drawn into local religious squabbles, insisting that spiritual conflicts be worked out among the tribal priests. This was the reason Pontius Pilate was so reluctant to hear the case against Jesus. Caesar had no interest.

Rome's problem was not with Jesus or the Christians. It was with the Jews by any designation and their steadfast refusal to recognize either Caesar or any other Roman god as worthy of worship. For many years Rome was willing to tolerate the Jewish resistance so long as the Sanhedrin kept the Jewish people in line. In the years following Jesus's death, the empire experienced all the cycles of nature that bring about calamity such as drought and famine (Acts 11:27–28).

It soon became popular to believe that Rome was under a curse because their gods were offended that the government had not honored them by forcing their worship upon the Jews/ Christians, as had been the case with every prior nation Rome conquered. When the Romans attempted to coerce the Jewish Christians into worshipping their gods along with Yahweh/ Jesus, the believers refused and were persecuted—not because of their worship of Jesus but because they would not give equal homage to the local gods who were in charge of things such as the weather.

Were the Romans correct in their assumption that their gods were angry with the noncompliant Jews/Christians? Probably. At least if one believes what the Old Testament has to say about such matters. The Roman gods had different names but were otherwise not substantially different from the multiplicity of gods, those disobedient high-ranking angels, mentioned in the Torah and the Prophets.

Some argue that prophetic writings such as Jeremiah 2:11 and 5:7 declared that the other gods mentioned in the Scriptures were nothing. What Jeremiah meant was that they were nothing when compared to Yahweh. The prophets recognized that the idol gods could not save the people, but they could and did harass them.

> From our youth shameful gods have consumed the fruits of our fathers' labor—their flocks and herds, their sons and daughters.
>
> —JEREMIAH 3:24

While Colossians 2 tells us that at the cross Jesus made a public display (some translations say "laughing stock") of the celestial powers, principalities, and rulers, unfortunately, it does not tell us that He did anything to dislodge them any more than He destroyed Satan.

But why not? Would not the sacrifice of Jesus have been a superb opportunity for Yahweh to vanquish all His enemies, including the ancient demonic structures and Satan himself? What would the world look like if only He had?

Instead Satan was permitted to continue going freely about as a hungry lion seeking whom he could destroy, as 1 Peter 5:8 declares. History simply does not support that the "prince of this world" accepted his defeat and went away to lick his wounds in eternal obscurity. Rather it seems his ire was stoked, and he went mercilessly after the infant church. Through his demon gods and their human agents he persecuted the new believers ruthlessly—and in many places still does. Where were the holy angels who were loyal to Jesus all that time? Why did they not enter the battle? Why do we find no mention of a celestial siege against evil until the Book of Revelation? When will we see the wrath of the Lamb poured out against Satan, as our theology demands?

Unfortunately, the New Testament ends without giving us a satisfactory answer.

Chapter 7

WHY DID JESUS ESTABLISH
THE CHURCH?

B EFORE WE ANSWER the question serving as the title of
this chapter, perhaps we should first ask, "*Did* Jesus
establish the church?" It is popular to hear some mod-
ernists argue that Jesus never intended to set up a new religion.
I would argue that is precisely what He meant to do. Religion
is defined by Encarta as "a set of strongly-held beliefs, values,
and attitudes that somebody lives by."[1] No matter how loudly

we sing about freeing ourselves from religion, it is impossible to do so.

Every person lives by religious conviction, an internal compass that governs how we do things. Jesus told us to repent—to change our minds—about religion, not to abandon it. Jesus established the church to do one thing: undo the works of the devil.

> His intent was that now, through the church, the manifold wisdom of God should be made known to the rulers and authorities in the heavenly realms.
>
> —EPHESIANS 3:10

Matthew 16 tells of the day Jesus took the disciples to a region near Caesarea Philippi, climbed on top of a rock in front of a cave, and asked the question, "Who do you say that I am?" The place Jesus chose to ask this paradigm-altering question had long been associated with pagan worship and sacrifice.[2]

In all likelihood the disciples would have experienced the same spiritual discomfort as any other Jew who entered such a religiously desecrated area. Local legend held that the cave was the entry point to the netherworld. It was as if Jesus intentionally crossed an unseen barrier where worship associated with demon gods was rampant and unchallenged and then stood up on the doorstep of Hades and tossed down a gauntlet to His men.

When Peter made his confession that Jesus was the Messiah and the Son of the living God, the rules of engagement between the warring worlds of the spirit realm shifted. After affirming that flesh and blood had not revealed this to Peter but God Himself had, Jesus announced that the scope of the battle would now change.

> Upon this rock, I will build My church; and the gates of Hades will not overpower it.
>
> —MATTHEW 16:18, NAS

Some say Jesus referred to building on the rock as a parody of words because Peter, or *Petra*, means rock. While this may be true, it seems more important that Jesus was announcing the establishment of the church on a rock-solid foundation at the entrance to Hades. The disciples would not have understood this to be a declaration against the work of the evil one, but Satan most certainly would have.

How might Satan have felt about what Jesus did? I suggest that the prince of this world was most likely insulted. After all, from the time Jesus rose from the baptismal waters of the Jordan River Satan had tried to force an altercation with Him. When Satan found Jesus alone in the desert, he tried to tempt Him, appeal to His ego, and finally to bargain with Him.

How did Jesus respond to Satan's approach? Somewhat dismissively. While it is true that Jesus responded to the devil's challenges by quoting Scripture according to Luke 4, He avoided emotional engagement. Jesus did not bind him, cast him out, send him to the abyss, curse him, challenge him, or malign him in any way. Perhaps we should not attempt to do this either.

As John Paul Jackson wrote in *Needless Casualties of War*, "When contending with the devil, Jesus spoke firmly but with the utmost respect. He did not revile when answering Satan's temptations. Nor did Jesus speak rudely, disrespectfully, or call Satan demeaning names. Rather, Jesus simply quoted Scripture to rebuke the devil."[3] When the whole world might have been different if only Jesus had slain malevolence with one word, there must be a reason He did not.

Satan knew who Jesus was and why He had become incarnate. No doubt he recognized Him, and because he can read and quote Scripture, Satan understood from the Prophets and Psalms that a redeemer was coming who would pay the price for the redemption of humanity by death on a cross. Psalm 22 reads like an eyewitness account to this future event.

From the time Jesus appeared on the earth, contrary to what many have thought, Satan's goal was to prevent Him from going to the cross, not to send Him there. When Satan could not make a treaty with Jesus in the desert, his right to rule over the world hung in the balance. If Jesus reached His goal at the cross, Satan's authority to govern the kingdoms of the earth would be canceled. He had to make a deal with the Son of God or have Him killed in some other way. He tried to do both.

When Jesus refused to interact with Satan in a serious, personal confrontation, the fallen archangel may have been genuinely confused. Jesus's announcement about the establishment of the church at Caesarea Philippi was made as much for Satan's hearing as the disciples'. Until then Satan's rampage over the earth had been immense and without challenge.

Boyd explains it like this: "As the Gospels portray it, this demonic alien army is vast in number and global in influence. The sheer number of possessions recorded in the Gospels, the large number of multiple possessions recorded, and many allusions to vast numbers of people who were possessed reveal the belief that the number of evil spirits was indefinitely large. The world was understood to be saturated with demons, whose destructive influence was all-pervasive. Everything about Jesus's ministry informs us that He judged every feature of the world that was not in keeping with the Creator's all-good design as being directly or indirectly the result of this invading presence."[4]

When Jesus announced that the church—mere human beings—would somehow overcome the works of evil no matter how the gates of Hades resisted, Satan would have been blindsided. How could this be? Satan knew every word of the Law, the Psalms, and the Prophets, and in them was no clue that such a thing as the church was coming. The adage that everything revealed in the New Testament is concealed in the Old Testament is largely true, except for the church.

The mystery, God's wisdom as Paul declared in Romans 16:25, that had been hidden and destined for our glory before time began was the church. Whatever the *ecclesia* was in Satan's mind, it was to be built on his perceived frailty of mankind. He must have regarded Jesus's words as insulting to his power, much the same way Goliath was enraged that the armies of Israel would send a mere boy to challenge him.

IS IT THE JOB OF THE CHURCH TO COMBAT EVIL?

Some would say that combating evil is the primary job of the church. According to Ephesians 3:10 the church is the only institution on the planet authorized to combat evil at its source: the rulers and authorities in the heavenly realms, of which the chief antagonist is Satan. Jesus's instructions to the disciples were clear.

> Heal the sick, raise the dead, cleanse the lepers, cast out demons. Freely you received, freely give.
>
> —MATTHEW 10:8, NAS

Boyd writes: "It is crucial for us to recognize that Jesus's view about the rule of Satan and the pervasive influence of his army was not simply a marginal piece of first-century apocalyptic thought that he happened to embrace. It is, rather, the driving force behind everything Jesus says and does."[5] He never appealed to some mysterious divine will to explain why a person was ill, maimed, or tormented as some in the modern church are prone to do. In every instance He spoke of these conditions as consequences of a creation gone berserk through the influence of Satan's army of demons.

The Gospels are replete with examples of Jesus declaring sickness to be the work of the devil, never once attributing disease to be a tool in God's hands to somehow better the human condition. He treated sick people as casualties of war; the church should have the same attitude. Sick people should never be subjected to accusations that they are somehow responsible for their conditions because of sins of omission, commission, or lack of faith.

If the church seems reluctant to lay claim to being able to heal the sick, it is with good reason. It so seldom seems to work. While it is well attested to that prayer can dramatically aid in the healing process, the testimonies of merely laying hands on people and seeing immediate release and recovery from debilitating illness are rare. If Jesus's command to the disciples to "heal the sick" is still relevant, should we understand it differently two thousand years later?

WHAT DID JESUS MEAN?

In John 14:12 Jesus told the disciples they would do greater things than He had done. Pause and consider the implausibility that human beings could actually do that—greater things than the second person of the Trinity. But suppose we were willing to reconsider Jesus's words through current revelation, thereby shifting the paradigm through which we might imagine the magnitude of what He was authorizing His followers to accomplish.

While Jesus's words are eternal, if they are *living* words, then they must expand and change in practical application to the environment they are in now, as do all living things. We can deprive ourselves of the power of the gospel by too narrowly defining what words mean. Let me offer an example.

Dan and Diane Morstad have been the directors of a counseling center in Minnesota for more than two decades. Early in their ministry it was prophesied to them that one day they would buy their own building. "You will know it is what God has for you because it will be filled with windows," the prophet said. Through the years they moved a number of times but never found the right place to buy.

Finally a perfect opportunity presented itself. The only problem was the building was almost completely devoid of windows. Nonetheless, it suited their needs and was within their price range. Somewhat reluctantly they made an offer that was accepted. Soon after closing the sale, Diane wandered through the building to take a look at all the work being done in the various cubicles. Suddenly she had an epiphany. On every desk was a computer opened to the Windows operating system. The building was literally filled with windows.

Every instance of Jesus's healing is reported as a one-on-one encounter with Him. Either the sick person was brought to Him, or someone on behalf of an infirmed asked Jesus to do something about his predicament. No doubt there were occasions when He might have healed throngs of people all at one time. While the same practice of praying for the sick or laying on of hands is a valid part of the church today, it simply does not fit the description of being a greater thing than Jesus did.

Suppose instead of viewing the advance of biotechnology and medicine as threats to the sovereignty of God, as some Christians are unfortunately prone to do, the church began to see them as instruments of spiritual warfare. Imagine that the gift of healing might not be limited to those who can pray but is also resident in the minds of pathologists and contagious disease specialists in laboratories where vaccines and antidotes for all kinds of cancer and other chronic, devouring diseases could be developed.

Suppose the church began to fund and encourage medical research the way it does missions. Its healing mandate would no longer be limited to those who were able to stand in a prayer line. Entire nations might be healed, and the most pervasive manifestations of Satan could be contained or eradicated. Such an accomplishment meets the bar of being a greater thing than Jesus did and raises the medical arts to a forceful tool to combat evil.

DELIVERANCE FROM EVIL SPIRITS

Evil spirits also afflict people in ways that cannot be combated with medicine. But not all evil spirits are created equal and thus cannot be addressed in a one-size-fits-all fashion. To do so can sometimes leave a victim in worse condition than before. We know from Ephesians 3 and other places in Scripture that there is a hierarchy of evil: thrones, powers, principalities, princes (Lucifer and the archangel over Persia are two examples), and more modern descriptors such as cosmic-level and terrestrial evil.

Although Jesus could have done so, there is no mention in the New Testament that Jesus ever confronted an evil spirit outside of the terrestrial paradigm. We will consider the higher levels of the hierarchy in a later chapter. For now let's consider those whom Jesus called out or cast out—evil spirits operating in the earthly realm where mankind has been given authority. Chapter 8 will discuss demon gods who operate in a different plane of reality.

This book does not propose to spend an inordinate amount of time on the ministry of deliverance. For an advanced study of deliverance, I recommend the writings of Doris Wagner, Edward Murphy, Derek Prince, or Rebecca Greenwood, among others. Nonetheless we must touch on Jesus's command to cast out demons in order to differentiate between terrestrial and cosmic-level spiritual activity.

Consistent with ideas advanced by Bible teacher Francis McNutt, I broadly categorize evil spirits in three ways: menacing, carnal, and demonic. I prefer the term "deliverance" to "exorcism" because one is to the other as algebra I is to calculus. The task of a deliverance minister is to do the work Jesus gave the church. The job of an exorcist is to deal with powerful demons that have legally gained complete control of a person's mind and will such that the victim is no longer able to act independently. Possession is a rare occurrence.

For centuries the Catholic church has been the most widely recognized institution in developing the protocol for training exorcists as opposed to deliverance ministers. To the dismay of some, in recent decades there has been less emphasis by the Catholic church on the rite of exorcism. Malachi Martin expresses his concern in *Hostage to the Devil*: "In the Roman Catholic Church, the Order of the Exorcist—part of every priest's ordination since time immemorial—has been omitted from the new rite of priestly ordination, as drawn up by innovators after 1964 in the wake of the Second Vatican Council."[6]

Perhaps the most common form of spiritual harassment comes through menacing spirits: low-level, one-aspect entities that gain access to a person through an injury to the soul. An *aspect* is what the spirit *does* or how it is identified by what it causes in its host's behavior. While the afflicted person may demonstrate antisocial behavior, it is important to remember that he or she is a victim of abuse and is not responsible for what has happened to him or her.

Typical causes for wounded souls are child abuse, exposure to pornography at an early age, abandonment, rejection, trauma, sexual abuse, battering, and psychological torture. Therefore the name of the attaching spirit might be lust, fear, shame, and so forth. The intruders manifest in behavior associated with social or relational dysfunction.

Menacing spirits hide and sometimes cause the victim to

hide with them in the form of an alternate personality. In severe cases a trained psychologist is often needed as part of the ministry team.

Menacing spirits can be contained, but no attempt to cast them out should be made. A deliverance minister friend, who requested anonymity, describes these spirits as resembling fish hooks that latch into the wound in the victim's psyche or soul. If there is an attempt to cast it out, the hook does further damage to the injury, just as jerking a hook from the mouth of the fish rips the flesh. The ministry in this situation is light and love. When the cause of the hurt is exposed, the light and love of Jesus (the ministry of the church) will cause a natural healing process to begin. Through therapy and prayer the wound heals, and the spirit has no place to hang on and departs on its own.

Carnal spirits are not necessarily single-aspect spirits though they are usually addressed as such. These spirits gain entry to the soul through repeated, intentional sin. The usual suspects are drugs, unrestrained sex, pornography, lust, brutality, cruelty, infidelity, etc. The church is likely to encounter persons with carnal obsession in divorce courts, jails, hospitals, or as attempted suicides—in other words, at the point of crisis.

The victim must want help and generally does not until the consequences of his or her behavior have created an untenable situation. Carnal spirits delight in the behavior they cause and may take years to detect because they want to remain hidden as long as possible. Jackson writes, "The better they are at hiding their presence, the stronger and more entrenched they become. Their goal is to remain within a person until the person's influence is overcome, the person has fulfilled demonically inspired tasks of harming, wounding, and destroying others, or the person is dead."[7]

A first deliverance attempt usually ends unsuccessfully because the person does not want true deliverance from the sin that both he and the spirit take pleasure in. He only wants deliverance from the crisis in which he currently finds himself. Clichés such as "he has to hit bottom" are generally true. Rarely is a person delivered from drunkenness at his first DUI hearing. It is not until he or she violates probation for the third or fourth time and faces jail that genuine repentance and healing are sought. Carnal spirits may be cast out, but an attempt to do so generally does not work until the victim has exhausted all other options and seeks true deliverance. A therapist, as well as a minister, is generally needed for successful rehabilitation.

The third category is demonic spirits or, as Martin describes them, "possessing spirits." Martin writes, "Nor does one become possessed suddenly, the way one might break an arm or catch the measles. Rather, possession is an ongoing *process*. A process that affects the two faculties of the soul: the mind, by which an individual receives and internalizes knowledge. And the will, by which an individual chooses to act upon that knowledge."[8]

People do not become possessed by accident. There are what Martin refers to as "disposing factors" present that always include conscious, intentional dabbling into occult practices. A trained exorcist looks for specific behavior that signals a possessing spirit.

A peculiar revulsion to symbols and truths of religions is always without exception a mark of the possessed person. In the verification of a case of demon possession by Church authorities, this "symptom" of revulsion is triangulated with other physical phenomena frequently associated with possession—the inexplicable stench; freezing temperature; telepathic powers about purely religious and moral matters; a peculiarly unlined or completely smooth or stretched skin, or unusual distortion of the face…"possessed gravity" (the possessed person becomes physically immovable, or those around the person are weighted down with suffocating pressure); levitation (the possessed rises and floats off the ground, chair, or bed; there is no physically traceable support); violent smashing of furniture, constant opening and slamming doors, tearing of fabric in the vicinity of the possessed, without a hand laid on them; and so on.[9]

If the person continues along this path, the possibility of "perfect possession" increases. "As the term implies, a victim of perfect possession is absolutely controlled by evil and gives no outward indication, no hint whatsoever, of the demonic residing within. He or she will not cringe, as others who are possessed will, at the sight of such religious symbols as a crucifix or a rosary. The perfectly possessed will not bridle at the touch of holy water, nor hesitate to discuss religious topics with equanimity."[10]

Jesus encountered and addressed all three types of demonic spirits. Mark 1 tells what happened one day in a synagogue.

> Just then there was a man in their synagogue with an unclean spirit; and he cried out, saying, "What business do we have with each other, Jesus of Nazareth? Have You come to destroy us? I know who You are—the Holy One of God!" And Jesus rebuked him, saying, "Be quiet, and come out of him!" Throwing him into convulsions, the unclean spirit cried out with a loud voice and came out of him.
>
> —MARK 1:23–26, NAS

Evil spirits of this kind call Jesus by name and expect Him to destroy them. They come out with violence and screaming, often harming their host in the exit by throwing him or her into convulsions and, on at least one occasion, into the fire. An amazing story is told in Mark 5 about a man who was infested with thousands of spirits who named themselves "Legion." When Jesus ordered the spirits out, they begged Him to send them into a herd of pigs, to which Jesus agreed. Why? It could be because they offered to go without a fight. A multitude of evil spirits exiting all at one time could easily kill the person.

Where do these invading spirits come from? Why would the supernatural desire to inhabit something with the limitations of flesh and blood? There are many theories, and I recommend readers consider them all while keeping in mind that the best answers we have are still disputable. Most scholars do not equate demonic gods (disobedient angels) with the spiritual/demonic invasion Jesus told His disciples to cast out.

There is no support from Scripture that angels desire to inhabit human bodies or that they become a different entity other than what they were created to be. Some respected deliverance ministers such as the late Derek Prince have speculated that they may be the disembodied spirits of a pre-Adamic race. Whatever their source, how might we envision how invasion of evil occurs in human beings?

Imagine that occupying spirits exist and infect the world in the same way viruses and bacteria exist. Menacing spirits are drawn to wounded, bleeding souls just as flies are drawn to road kill. Carnal spirits are drawn to those whose warped psyche takes pleasure in the perverse.

Neither type intentionally destroys their human hosts, though such may be the outcome, because they cannot survive without one. Most deliverance ministers are trained to be on guard that demonic spirits can and do move from one person to another during an exorcism. Both are evil and are subject to deliverance ministry because they are subject to Jesus. When Jesus encountered someone plagued by this type of spirit, He took pity and cast it out, but He made no attempt to destroy it.

Some deliverance ministers command the invading spirit to "go to the foot of the cross" or some other place, and while this may work, it does not have a precedent in the New Testament. Could it be that menacing and carnal spirits are entities lost in the warp of time? If Prince was onto something about the origin of these spirits, rather than originating from a pre-Adamic race, could they perhaps be a remnant supernatural DNA of a hybrid race that was never intended—the Nephlim?

If so, they may be like lost ghosts caught between worlds. They must find a host in flesh and blood. They cannot repent, and they are of no value to Satan because the prince of darkness has little interest in manipulating inferior, mutant spirits to torment humans for sport, as it does not advance his primary purpose. His war is and has always been with God. Men and women who live with the level of spiritual significance to garner the personal attention of Lucifer himself are very few.

Still, menacing and carnal alone do not sufficiently describe all the evil spirits Jesus encountered and cast out. He also treated sickness as if it were demonic in nature. We have already discussed the evolution of Jesus's mandate to "heal the sick" through the medical arts. The conundrum is, if we are to cast out demonic spirits of disease, why does it so seldom work?

In the charismatically inclined body of believers, it is common practice to try to bind and cast out infirmities such as cancer, diabetes, scleroses, and other debilitating conditions. I asked my friend Doris Wagner, perhaps one of the most respected deliverance ministers in the country, why we do not see more success. These are her words:

> In only one instance have I come across a "spirit of cancer" I was able to eject. Otherwise I have no answer as to why cancer, diabetes, or other chronic ailments are usually not responsive to prayer or deliverance, as we have seen. But occasionally there is a miracle, and these diseases are totally healed, for which we are grateful. We always pray and ask anyway.
>
> It seems like some diseases such as certain cancers and autism are very difficult, not to say almost impossible, to deal with. Since I am somewhat close to the autism community, I have heard of only one case of a boy healed of autism, and that was in Brazil, but I have not had a chance to check it out. The story I got is that he suddenly began to talk when previously he

had been nonverbal. I don't know how healed he may be in other areas. I have another friend in Louisiana whose son was autistic, and they claimed healing, but it is certainly not total healing. However, this boy is very functional and will probably be able to handle life just fine.[11]

While there is anecdotal evidence that deliverance prayer over devastating diseases sometimes works, in most cases it does not. If it did, there would not be the widespread presence of these conditions in the church. I personally know several highly respected ministers of deliverance whose reputation for ridding people of menacing and carnal spirits is well known. Most, however, do not have the same record of success in casting out disease as they have with other spirits. In fact, many suffer from the very illnesses they try to cast out of others. I asked Doris what she thought about this perplexity.

This is a tough one for which I have no answer. However, not to pray for someone else when a person is gifted to do so might just be a sin. I have the grace to handle a tough, painful existence, joking to Peter that I am only handicapped from the neck down, and that the rest still works just fine. I am now confined to a scooter or wheelchair. To feel sorry for myself and make everyone else around me miserable would be very counterproductive. To pray for someone else and see them helped is a blessing and to demand anything from a loving God is not right for me.[12]

Doris Wagner may be the bravest woman I know. I agree with her that deliverance ministry for chronic disease should continue if for no other reason than it sometimes works. But it does not always, and we do not know why.

Jesus established the church as a kingdom with governmental authority to displace another kingdom whose leader had seized control of the earth. I suspect that not only was Satan confused by Jesus's announcement to establish a church against his empire, but so were the disciples since they had no notion of what a church was. The word Jesus used was *ecclesia*, a term associated with the Roman senate. One might ask why He did not say He would establish a temple or a synagogue.

An institution of government seems an odd analogy for the disposition of spiritual matters. Perhaps it was because, as C. Peter Wagner has been known to say, "it takes a government to overthrow a government." In the same way it is not lawful for a citizen of this country to declare war against another country; an individual believer, regardless of his spiritual fervor, cannot wage war against the kingdom of evil. Job, no matter how righteous, was no match for the empire ruled by Leviathan.

Whatever else the work of the church might be, it must be primarily about reversing the control of evil in people and every aspect of society if the knowledge of God is to cover the earth as the "waters cover the sea" (Isa. 11:9; Hab. 2:14). What a logical and beautiful path forward this might have been for mankind if only Jesus had destroyed Satan and the lesser gods at the cross. Unfortunately, He did not. The question then becomes, why not?

Chapter 8

LESSER GODS

THE DEMON GODS represent a far greater threat to people than displaced, earthbound spirit remnants of the Nephilim (if indeed that is their origin). These are the archangels who once exercised power over the nations as helpers to mankind, as the Septuagint's version of Deuteronomy 32:7–9 declares, but who subsequently disobeyed and lost their positions of authority. These angels cannot be the same ones who rebelled with Lucifer, or else they would never have been given governing roles over the earth. How they became organized into the demonic hierarchy of princes, thrones, principalities, and the rest organized under Lucifer's rule is unclear from the Bible.

Their fall from grace began when they received worship from people who sought their help as mediators between themselves and God. Soon they abused their charge over humanity (Ps. 82) and became demon gods. Justin Martyr explains what happened. "But the angels transgressed this appointment...they afterwards subdued the human race to themselves...and among men they sowed murders, wars, adulteries, intemperate deeds, and all wickedness."[1] What is puzzling is, why did they do it? What drove powerful and glorious beings to put their royal position at risk by engaging in forbidden behavior?

Perhaps they underestimated the seduction of worship. Among celestial beings, worship appears to have the effect of an aphrodisiac. Satan himself was willing to hand over all the kingdoms of the world to Jesus without a fight if the Son of Man would do one thing: worship him. Perhaps the clearest and utterly nonnegotiable command from the beginning of the Bible to the end is that all in heaven and earth are to worship only the one true God—and Him alone.

How can we understand the lure of adoration? Let me offer an analogy. When I managed a television station in Jacksonville, Florida, several years ago, the news department produced a five-part series on the drug problem in the state and the seemingly futile attempts by law enforcement to control it. A part of the investigation had to do with the use of cocaine and its derivatives among the well-to-do. One day I interviewed a doctor who agreed to be on camera in silhouette (face and voice disguised) as a professional who almost destroyed his career by using cocaine.

"Why were you willing to risk your reputation, career, family—your entire life—for an illegal drug when as a physician, all sorts of legal mood-altering substances are readily available to you without consequence?" I asked.

I have never forgotten what he said. "Cocaine has attributes other drugs do not have. It draws you in emotionally. I literally fell in love with cocaine. I would have sold my soul to possess it."

I learned from his and subsequent interviews with others that cocaine is unique in the world of narcotics in that it captures the soul as well as the body. Perhaps the desire for worship is something like that. Once it is experienced, it becomes impossible to resist.

All that we reliably know about angels comes from the Bible. Whatever else they might be like, they seem to share many attributes with humans. They are self-willed, intelligent, emotional, ambitious, and curious (1 Pet. 1:12). They belong to a hierarchy (ministering spirits, archangels, seraphim, cherubim). They sing, praise, talk, fight among themselves (as did Michael and the prince of Persia), contend with humans (as did Jacob and the angel of the Lord), and counsel with God. Some believe angels are fascinated with women (Gen. 6), especially their hair (1 Cor. 11:10, 15). Scripture presents all named angels as male; however, this opinion does not explain the female idols of pagan religion.

When ancient people became aware of the heavenly beings

that were watching over them, it would have been a natural next step to petition the angels for assistance or favor. It is not hard to imagine how offers of sacrifice and promises of devotion and flattery might blend together to tempt the angels to go beyond their prescribed limits of human interaction. Perhaps adoration from humans became so addictive that what began as granting special help to someone as a reward for his devotion soon morphed into punishing the person if worship was withheld. Jeremiah 3 says something like that.

> From our youth shameful gods have consumed the fruits of our fathers' labor—their flocks and herds, their sons and daughters.
>
> —Jeremiah 3:24

When the angels began mistreating humans as Psalm 82 indicates, the Lord Himself stepped in and rebuked them. But the Lord also rebuked the people for their part in the seduction.

> Why should I forgive you? Your children have forsaken me and sworn by gods that are not gods. I supplied all their needs, yet they committed adultery and thronged to the houses of prostitutes.
>
> —Jeremiah 5:7

Throughout the Old Testament Yahweh likened homage to other gods as prostitution. This illustrates the depth of emotion associated with the act of worship. It was not that Israel abandoned their allegiance to Him so much as that they dallied with false gods when they felt their needs were not being met. God used Jeremiah to speak a scathing rebuke for their infidelity.

> Will you steal and murder, commit adultery and perjury, burn incense to Baal and follow other gods you have not known, and then come and stand before me in this house, which bears my Name, and say, "We are safe"—safe to do all these detestable things? Has this house, which bears my Name, become a den of robbers to you?
>
> —JEREMIAH 7:9–11

Although the prophets described the worship of idols made of wood and stone as worthless things, it would be a mistake to assume they did not represent authentic power. The admonition of Yahweh appears more to be a comment on the ridiculous idea that celestial beings could ever be contained in vessels made by man rather than a statement that the idols did not represent actual entities.

It can be assumed that when the governing angels rebelled against God and people, God removed them from their positions of authority and banned them from the heavenly council. However, as we have seen with Lucifer, there is no evidence He revoked their powers or cast them out of the earth realm since they still await judgment (1 Cor. 6:3).

With them having no place else to go, it is entirely plausible that they submitted to the rule of Lucifer, the prince of this world, under whose command they would have been before his fall from heaven—a perfect case of the devil you know being preferable to the one you do not. Unlike Lucifer, whose interests in human beings was and is limited to their usefulness to him for a specific purpose, the lesser gods warred against people inflicting disease, calamity, and disaster out of revenge. They genuinely loathed people because it was the forbidden interaction with people that brought about their great fall. Two millennia after the cross not much has changed.

In the Old Testament Yahweh was clearly understood to reign supreme over the entire cosmic society of heaven and earth, but His sovereignty was never taken to imply that He was the only supernatural being. The ability of lesser gods to deceive people into worship of themselves was not merely a belief found in pagan religions but, as we have seen, was common in the Hebrew writings. Baal, Ashera, Astarte, Dagon, Chemosh, Tammuz, Mammon, and Artemis (Diana) were believed to be powerful gods who held influence over particular people groups and geography.

Some doctrine holds that there is only one God with real power in the cosmos and that the demon gods mentioned in the Old Testament were figments of the imagination of tribal people who needed a way to explain hardship. Their explanation for suffering is that God used plagues, famines, and natural disaster to teach people needed lessons. At best this seems disingenuous if we believe God said what the prophets claim He said. If biblical accounts concerning the ability of lesser gods to inflict calamity are not true, then the blame for all the evil in the universe falls squarely on Yahweh. How can God be taken seriously that His desire is to free people from the grip of evil, as the Bible insists, if He Himself is the cause of it?

Monotheism does not mean denying other gods exist. N. T. Wright argues, "The postulation of supernatural beings other than the one God has nothing to do with a declining away from 'pure' monotheism—or if it does, we must say that we have very few examples of 'pure' monotheism anywhere, including in the Hebrew Bible."[2]

Boyd writes, "Creational monotheism maintains that while Yahweh must genuinely battle with spiritual cosmic rivals, this 'must' is itself something Yahweh Himself has brought into being. It need not imply that Yahweh secretly controls His rivals, only the very power of His rivals to resist Him is given by Him."[3]

Is God the cause of His own problem? In a way, yes. The biblical pattern we see in how He gets things done lies in His willingness to share power with inferior beings of His own making. Yahweh's insistence on endowing self-willed, intelligent personalities with the ability to defy Him virtually assured that it would only be a matter of time until one of them decided to try it. Lucifer's rebellion triggered a perfect storm in the cosmos, and the whole world found itself caught up in the crossfire of a cosmic struggle.

The problem of evil had a beginning. Why did God not solve it right then? Why did He not respond in a way that would have insured the fewest casualties—by destroying the rebellious archangel right then in view of all of heaven? At a minimum, the wrath of an infinite God against a finite creature would have eliminated any possibilities of future rebellion.

If Yahweh was the creator of Lucifer, surely He did not intend for him to become evil. Something must have gone horribly wrong. The narrative from the Bible concerning Lucifer's rebellion against God is sparse, but it is all we have. To construct a history from the information available to us requires a fair amount of speculation and a good bit of grace for honest people who read the same stories but arrive at different conclusions.

For example, the Western interpretation that the snake that tempted Adam and Eve in the garden was Satan in disguise is not universally shared. Jewish commentary points out a fact so obvious it is amazing how we overlook or ignore it. "Unlike some later Jewish and Christian literature, Genesis does not identify the talking snake with Satan or any other demonic being."[4] Therefore, to make a case that the serpent was Satan, we have to look for evidence somewhere else. It is widely taught that Ezekiel 28 and Isaiah 14 give us the missing evidence to corroborate that it was indeed the fallen Lucifer who was in the Garden of Eden.

> You were in Eden, the garden of God. . . . You were the anointed cherub who covers, and I placed you there.
>
> —EZEKIEL 28:13–14, NAS

The next verses reveal what happened to the anointed cherub whom we understand to be Lucifer:

> You were blameless in your ways from the day you were created until unrighteousness was found in you. By the abundance of your trade you were internally filled with violence, and you sinned; therefore I have cast you as profane from the mountain of God. And I have destroyed you, O covering cherub, from the midst of the stones of fire.
>
> —EZEKIEL 28:15–16, NAS

While some contend that this lament was intended toward the king of Tyre and no one else, it is hard to imagine why Ezekiel would have referred to a human king as an anointed cherub who was in the garden. What was the sin that caused Lucifer's exile? Isaiah writes something similar.

> How you have fallen from heaven, O star of the morning, son of the dawn! You have been cut down to the earth, you who have weakened the nations! But you said in your heart, "I will ascend to heaven; I will raise my throne above the stars of God, and I will sit on the mount of assembly in the recesses of the north. I will ascend above the heights of the clouds; I will make myself like the Most High."
>
> —Isaiah 14:12–14, nas

If Isaiah were speaking only of the king of Babylon, why use such celestial language?

Why Did Lucifer Rebel?

I have asked this question of the most spiritually wise and theologically educated people I know. The answer has almost always been that pride drove Lucifer to covet Yahweh's throne. While pride may have fueled his rage, I doubt it was as simple as that. Lucifer's fury is more analogous to crimes of passion where spurned love and hateful jealousy are catalysts to acts of violence. There must be more to the story. Ezekiel 28 gives vivid detail of Lucifer's appearance:

> Every precious stone was your covering: the ruby, the topaz and the diamond; the beryl, the onyx and the jasper; the lapis lazuli, the turquoise and the emerald;

and the gold, the workmanship of your settings and
sockets, was in you. On the day that you were created
they were prepared.

—EZEKIEL 28:13, NAS

There are no other verses in the Bible describing angels
in such loving detail. All religions that acknowledge Lucifer
concur that God made him more splendid and with a higher
purpose than the cherubim, seraphim, or other archangels. Of
all the heavenly host, Lucifer was the closest to the heart of
God.

To understand his tragic rebellion, we must first consider
another celestial mystery—the Trinity, three Gods in one:
Father, Son, and Holy Spirit. John 1 tells us that in the beginning the Word (Jesus) was with God and the Word was God.
John 3 goes on to say that Jesus was the *begotten* Son of God,
not *made* by God as was the rest of creation.

Begotten means brought forth out of the same substance.
We believe Jesus the Son and God the Father are one, and yet
they are distinctive in their roles and presence. For example,
Yahweh was in heaven while Jesus was on the earth. Jesus said
He must go away before the Holy Spirit could come. Jesus
spoke of His Father in the third person. But at one time the
Father and the Son were together in one essence until God
the Father begat—brought forth out of Himself—God the
Son. Does Scripture offer any clues as to how or when this
might have happened?

Proverbs 8 has been embraced by many religions, including
New Age, because it seems to speak of the creation of an
ambiguous entity called Wisdom. However, revelation this

side of the cross has caused many scholars to look at the verses in a different light; Jesus and Wisdom are one and the same.

> The LORD brought me forth as the first of his works, before his deeds of old; I was appointed from eternity, from the beginning, before the world began. When there were no oceans, I was given birth, when there were no springs abounding with water; before the mountains were settled in place, before the hills, I was given birth, before he made the earth or its fields or any of the dust of the world.
>
> I was there when he set the heavens in place, when he marked out the horizon on the face of the deep, when he established the clouds above and fixed securely the fountains of the deep, when he gave the sea its boundary so the waters would not overstep his command, and when he marked out the foundations of the earth. Then I was the craftsman at his side. I was filled with delight day after day, rejoicing always in his presence, rejoicing in his whole world and delighting in mankind.
>
> Now then, my sons, listen to me; blessed are those who keep my ways. Listen to my instruction and be wise; do not ignore it. Blessed is the man who listens to me, watching daily at my doors, waiting at my doorway. For whoever finds me finds life and receives favor from the LORD. But whoever fails to find me harms himself; all who hate me love death.
>
> —PROVERBS 8:22–36

Isaiah 11 tells us that the spirit of wisdom would rest on the Messiah. Now consider the claims of the New Testament about Jesus compared with the words spoken by Wisdom.

Through him all things were made; without him nothing was made that has been made. In him was life, and that life was the light of men. The light shines in the darkness, but the darkness has not understood it.

—John 1:3–5

I am the light of the world. Whoever follows me will never walk in darkness, but will have the light of life.

—John 8:12

I tell you the truth, if anyone keeps my word, he will never see death.

—John 8:51

He who hates me hates my Father as well.

—John 15:23

He is the image of the invisible God, the firstborn over all creation. For by him all things were created: things in heaven and on earth, visible and invisible, whether thrones or powers or rulers or authorities; all things were created by him and for him. He is before all things, and in him all things hold together.

—Colossians 1:15–17

Some commentators, such as Adam Clarke, Matthew Henry, Watchman Nee, and Calvinist theologian Isaac de La Peyrer have speculated there was a time when Jesus had His being within the person of Yahweh in much the same way that Eve's person was hidden in Adam before God separated them. Then one day God the Father begat His Son from out of His singular habitation to become a distinct Person, consistent with John 3:16.

It is arguable among these scholars and others that the Proverbs 8 verses attributed to Wisdom may indeed describe the oneness of God becoming the mystery of God the Father and God the Son. To interpret the passages differently is to suggest that rather than being a characteristic of Jesus, the Wisdom described here is another distinct being sharing in the creation process. Indeed, a popular feminist movement in the 1990s claimed the Wisdom in Proverbs 8 was a separate feminine deity named Sophia (Greek term for *wisdom*) who shared in the divine nature of the Trinity.

The Greek word for "begotten" (*monogenes*) means single of its kind.[5] If Jesus is the "begotten" Son of God as Scripture testifies, and today sits at the right hand of the Father as Acts 2:33; 7:55; Romans 8:34; and Hebrews 1:3 attest, common sense demands that at one time Father and Son were one being that was somehow different from what They are now. The impact on the cosmos of such an extraordinary occurrence would be hard to overstate. What would it mean, and to whom would it matter? Revelation 12 tells us that something happened that was so remarkable it caused a war between the angels. What might it have been?

Allow me to speculate. Suppose it was something like this. Before the transformation occurred, all of the Godhead resided in one entity. During this unknown period in eternity past the three-in-one God dwelt in heaven with all of the angels They had created, one of whom was Lucifer: the seal of perfection, full of wisdom and perfect in beauty—the closest to the heart of God (Ezek. 28:12) and the one for whom there were no rivals for God's affection. Then everything changed. Adonai (Jesus) came forth from Yahweh's (God the Father) breast as a unique being.

Suddenly there was someone between Yahweh and Lucifer. The archangel was outraged and consumed by jealousy. "I will ascend to heaven; I will raise my throne above the stars of God. I will make my throne like that of the Most High," he boasted.

Suppose the throne Lucifer coveted was not that of Yahweh the Father but rather that of Adonai the Son. Perhaps Lucifer did not lust to be God the Father; he yearned to be the Son. Yet for all his splendor he could never be more than a created being. Adonai alone was true God of true God, one in being with the Father, begotten, not made. In jealousy and wrath Lucifer railed against heaven and earth, and the cosmos broke out in war.

When Jesus paid the debt of mankind to redeem us from the slavery of Satan's kingdom, He repudiated the rule of evil by the establishment of the church. With the fury of a spurned lover, Satan's offense was to grow all the more when he learned that the eternal destiny for the church was something he never imagined. The church would be the bride.

Chapter 9

THE WEAPONS OF WARFARE—
PROCEED WITH CAUTION

Satan, I bind you up and put you under my feet. I dance on your head and send you back to the fiery pit." As the woman continued to march around the room, berating and threatening Satan, the rest of the group jumped to their feet and began stomping on the Oriental rug chanting, "He is under my feet. Satan is under my feet."

I inched toward the door planning my escape in case things got worse, which they soon did. Getting between me and the door, they began dancing a circle around me, pointing at my Michael Kors patent pumps and singing, "He is under your feet. Satan is under your feet." I restrained my urge to cry out, "No, he is not under my feet, and he is not under yours either. Please do not pull on the dragon's tail." But since I was the guest speaker that night, I knew it would be embarrassing to the pastor who had invited me, so I composed myself and waited for it to be over.

Intercession Is Different

Intercession and prayer are not the same things. Intercession opens and closes portals on a spiritual plane. Everyone is called to pray, but not everyone is called to be an intercessor. The majority of intercessors operate in a true calling that helps make the world safe for the rest of us, but there are others who are presumptuous, untrained, and uncurbed who sometimes step beyond their boundaries and open gateways that should remain shut.

Jesus's admonition to the disciples in Luke 10:20 not to rejoice that the demons were subject to them means much more than we think it does. The most powerful weapons to displace evil and free people from its grip to advance the purposes of Jesus are intercessory prayer and corporate worship. But these same armaments in the mouths of passionate, fearless, but uninformed and unrestrained intercessors and singers who do not weigh the consequences of the words they use are akin to placing an AK-47 in the hands of a three-year-old.

Within the past few years a minister in charismatic circles

well known for warfare prayer and public decrees to "tear down strongholds and bind Satan" died suddenly on stage in front of hundreds of people. Some have privately wondered if the untimely death was related to the ministry method itself. More and more spiritual leaders are beginning to question whether prayer assaults against idolatrous structures are dangerous for most people and are better left to those specifically called and ordained for such a mission.

Pastor Barbara J. Yoder, the founding apostle and senior pastor of Shekinah Christian Church, known for her cutting-edge prophetic ministry and apostolic gifting, is also concerned about intercessors who go beyond their assigned spheres. (Some details in Yoder's accounts below have been changed to protect the identity of those involved.)

> I knew a young person years ago who was engaged in "spiritual warfare." He met with me, and I warned him of taking on Freemasonry directly. Apparently he also consulted another prophetic leader, and he cautioned him as well. He took it on anyway and was found dead at the age of thirty-five under mysterious circumstances. It was a very strange incident.
>
> I had felt he was in dangerous territory. Though I have not said so publicly, I have known of those who have died dealing in dangerous areas ignorantly.
>
> Years ago, shortly before a prominent leader fell, he had been ministering in a city where the whole evening was spent addressing demons over the territory and telling them to come down. I've never forgotten that.
>
> I also had a very strange experience in another city once. I preached at a church where their entire

worship service was spent addressing demons. I had a vision where the more they yelled at the devil, the more demons were attracted to surround and capture the church. By the time they were finished, the place was oppressive.[1]

To borrow an analogy from Mark Twain, the difference between knowledgeable intercession and rampant prayer that knows no boundaries is the difference between electricity and a lightning bolt. One illuminates; the other blows something up. Spoken prayer requires the use of words, and words have consequences. Nations go to war over words. Relationships are formed and destroyed through words (James 3:9). According to Genesis, God created the heavens and earth through the spoken word. The power of life and death is in the tongue (Prov. 18:21). James paints a vivid picture of the power of speech.

> A word out of your mouth may seem of no account, but it can accomplish nearly anything—or destroy it! It only takes a spark, remember, to set off a forest fire. A careless or wrongly placed word out of your mouth can do that. By our speech we can ruin the world, turn harmony to chaos, throw mud on a reputation, send the whole world up in smoke and go up in smoke with it, smoke right from the pit of hell.
>
> —James 3:5–6, The Message

Perhaps the rationale behind the biblical affirmation to pray in tongues is to avoid the repercussions of poorly chosen language in urgent matters of spiritual importance (1 Cor. 14:2). We will consider in more detail the use of prayer language in chapter 13. Jesus warned people that on the Day of Judgment they would give account for every careless word spoken (Matt. 12:36).

When Jesus encountered Satan face-to-face, there were many ways in which He could have addressed him. He could have cursed, maligned, or destroyed him, but He did not. Instead Jesus chose His words carefully. The argument that Jesus was modeling a way for us to use Scripture in confronting evil may be true, but there are hundreds of other verses He could have used that would have destroyed Satan and ended the problem of evil once and for all. Since Jesus did not slay him by word or deed, the question becomes, why not?

At the moment Jesus decided with His Father to become incarnate, He also implicitly agreed to obey the laws that governed the rest of flesh and blood. For example, He became subject to gravity. He had to eat, drink, and sleep. He also conformed to spiritual protocol when it came to high-ranking celestial beings. Although He knew their names and their hold over the people of the earth, He never addressed them directly. He limited His interaction to terrestrial demonic spirits who had invaded the lives of individuals. Jesus did not hunt down the demon gods, bind them up, call them out, or cast them down. Since He could have but did not, perhaps intercessors should not try to do it either.

Leanne Payne in her book *Listening Prayer* describes her encounters with intercessors who attempt to bind principalities and powers. "Thinking themselves to be intercessors extraordinaire and the only ones 'doing' spiritual warfare, they were actually practicing the presence of demons. They had drawn the attention of dark powers toward the Body of Christ by praying to them and through pridefully seeing themselves as 'binding' them.... Needless to say, we were brought into a spiritual conflict of unusual proportions, one that never should have occurred."[2]

John Paul Jackson has often cautioned believers about the audacity of challenging Satan. He tells of how the Lord chastised him about provoking Satan through the words of Job 41.

> Or can you pull in the sea beast, Leviathan, with a fly rod and stuff him in your creel? Can you lasso him with a rope, or snag him with an anchor? Will he beg you over and over for mercy, or flatter you with flowery speech? Will he apply for a job with you to run errands and serve you the rest of your life? Will you play with him as if he were a pet goldfish? Will you make him the mascot of the neighborhood children? Will you put him on display in the market and have shoppers haggle over the price? Could you shoot him full of arrows like a pincushion, or drive harpoons into his huge head? If you so much as lay a hand on him, you won't live to tell the story. What hope would you have with such a creature? Why, one look at him would do you in!
>
> —Job 41:1–9, The Message

Jackson writes, "God's warning echoed in my spirit. 'Who are you to taunt Satan? Who are you to imagine that you can capture Satan? Who are you to make Satan your servant? Or tame Satan as if he were an animal? Or kill Satan by throwing harpoons…at him? To attempt such things is full of presumption, vain imagination and false hope.'"[3]

A Pact With the Devil

Is spiritual warfare biblical, and should we engage in it at all? Yes, probably, but we must remain within the realms of the authority given in the New Testament. Attempting direct communication with any celestial power, especially Satan himself, can lead us into cleverly worded entanglements from which it can be difficult to escape. If Adam and Eve, created in God's perfect likeness, could be trapped and their futures forever altered as a result of playing word games with Satan, what about the rest of us? Are we really so confident as to suppose that our spiritual prowess is superior to that of whom Jesus acknowledged as the prince of this world?

Scott Peck, respected psychiatrist and author, tells a story in his book *The People of the Lie* about a man who made a pact with the devil. George suffered from compulsive thoughts about accidents, all manner of calamity, and dying prematurely. For example, at the age of thirteen, he developed a fear that his grandmother would die unless he touched a certain rock every day. He was terrified and could not rest until he completed the daily ritual. After several months of treatment Peck noticed that his patient's countenance had changed, so he asked him if something had happened. He said:

> I made a pact with the devil. I mean, I really don't believe in the devil, but I had to do something, didn't I? So I made this agreement that if I did give in to my compulsion and go back, then the devil would see to it that my thought came true.... For instance, the other day I had this thought near Chapel Hill. *The next time you come this way you will drive over the embankment and be killed.* Ordinarily, of course, I would have stewed about it for a couple of hours, and finally I would have gone back to the embankment just to prove the thought wasn't true.... But having made this pact, you see, I couldn't go back. Because as part of the agreement, if I went back, the devil would see

to it that I did drive over the embankment and would be killed."[4]

As George's confession rolled out, he soon revealed that he had upped the bargain with Satan, including the life of his son as well. Peck recounts that at first he did not know how to respond to what his patient had said. For several minutes the two men sat in silence until George became agitated.

"Do you think that I'm bad?"

"I think that in making this pact with the devil you have done something that is bad. Something evil."

"But I haven't really done anything," George explained. "Don't you see?...It's all been in my mind, a figment of my imagination. I don't even believe in the devil. I don't believe in God, for that matter.... The devil's not real. So how can my pact be real?"

...[Peck replied,] "I don't know any more about the devil than you do. I don't know whether it's a he, she, or an it. I don't know whether the devil's corporeal, or whether it's a force, or whether it's just a concept. But it doesn't matter. The fact remains that whatever it is, you made a contract with it."[5]

Spiritual Protocol

The writings of the New Testament acknowledge a protocol in the spirit realm that makes a difference between casting out demonic spirits as Jesus did and instructed His disciples to do and reviling or confronting celestial dignitaries. An analogy with a current world event might help us gain perspective on the importance of a code of behavior when dealing with important people who represent spiritual standing even if they are tyrants.

In April 2011 the world's most hunted and hated criminal was apprehended and executed—Osama bin Laden. The body was immediately taken into custody on a naval ship where it was ceremoniously washed, wrapped in white linen, and solemnly dropped into the sea as Islamic prayers were read. This was all done in keeping with the proper procedures of burial in one of the world's major religion.

Despite the demands of journalists, politicians, and American citizens to see pictures of the body, none were permitted. Why bother to offer dignity to a tyrant who was responsible for the deaths of thousands of people in torturous ways with plans to slay thousands more? Willing to risk the wrath of the public, the United States government held to their decision to withhold what were surely gruesome pictures of the assassinated despot. The government made the correct decision. To desecrate the body of a religious icon by improper burial or public ridicule would have been tantamount to declaring war against Islam. An already complex, mercurial, political, and military situation could have been made much worse and could have exploded with worldwide casualties.

HEAPING ABUSE ON CELESTIAL BEINGS

The writers of the New Testament acknowledged a code of conduct concerning the angelic realm. For example, the apostle Peter is not usually noted for his keen spiritual discernment or tact, yet his epistle shows that he was well aware that deliverance as Jesus demonstrated it was not to be confused with the separate action of rebuking the lesser gods, which was prohibited. In warning the people about false prophets and teachers, he wrote:

> This is especially true of those who follow the cor-
> rupt desire of the sinful nature and despise authority.
> Bold and arrogant, these men are not afraid to slander
> celestial beings; yet even angels, although they are
> stronger and more powerful, do not bring slanderous
> accusations against such beings in the presence of the
> Lord. But these men blaspheme in matters they do
> not understand.
>
> —2 PETER 2:10–12

Not only does the Bible warn against humans rebuking Satan or other principalities and powers, but also it appears that not even angels themselves are allowed to rebuke Satan.

> In the very same way, these dreamers pollute their
> own bodies, reject authority and slander celestial
> beings. But even the archangel Michael, when he was
> disputing with the devil about the body of Moses, did
> not dare to bring a slanderous accusation against him,
> but said, "The Lord rebuke you!"
>
> —JUDE 8–9

We are warned in the New Testament to be alert and sober minded because Satan is a roaring lion roaming about seeking whom he may devour (1 Pet. 5:8). Although it is common Christian jargon, nowhere does the Bible say he is a toothless lion.

We are told to resist the devil, not to challenge him (James 4:7). How exactly is one supposed to do that? Paul acknowledges that our struggle is not against flesh and blood, but flesh and blood is often all we see. Just as the Holy Spirit needs a person to accomplish God's will on the earth, Satan is bound by the same need. He must also have the cooperation of a person. Think about the brutal executions and dismemberments of Daniel Pearl and the contractors in Iraq.

Unaided by external, supernatural malevolence that invades and controls higher mind functions, human beings created in God's perfect likeness are not capable of executing that level of horror. But the rulers, authorities, and powers—the lesser gods—in the heavenly realm most certainly are.

But does not Colossians 2:15 say that Jesus made a public display of the powers and principalities, disarming them at the cross? However this verse should be interpreted, it clearly does not mean the lesser gods have lost their power, just as Satan has not lost his. If these spirits were powerless, the world would not look the way that it does two thousand years after the cross.

While Jesus did not authorize us to launch a frontal attack against Satan and his cohorts, Ephesians 6 does admonish us to be prepared to stand against them by putting on the only armor available to us: the helmet of salvation, the breastplate of righteousness, the shoes of peace, the belt of truth, the shield of faith, and the sword of the Spirit (God's Word). The helmet is of particular use because it represents the knowledge of Jesus that protects our minds from counterfeit gospels. This is what Paul meant when he wrote in 2 Corinthians 10 that the weapons we fight with have the power to demolish strongholds, arguments, and pretensions that rise against the knowledge of God and enable us to take captive every thought to the obedience of Christ.

Strongholds are mind-sets, distorted ways of thinking that make us vulnerable to spiritual influences that lead to the destruction of self or others. All of us have one or several of them, and it is through these patterns of thinking that all new information must pass and be accepted or rejected based on whether it syncs with previously established thought. A wrong mind-set is almost impossible to discern by the person who holds it, particularly if it is a religious one. It is those mind-sets formed in religion that have accounted for some of humanity's most egregious acts of mass murder and mayhem in the name of God. Slaughter of native people, the Inquisition, the Crusades, the Holocaust, ethnic cleansing, the Salem witch hunts, Darfur, Myanmar—the list is numbing.

The Council at Lausanne

In November 1971 Billy Graham convened a meeting at which he inquired about the advisability of holding another international congress on world evangelization as a follow-up to the 1966 World Congress on Evangelism in Berlin. The purpose of the meeting was to gather the leaders of evangelical Protestant Christians from across the globe for strategic planning, inspiration, and fellowship. Lausanne, Switzerland, was named as the site of the congress. A topic of primary interest in the first and subsequent meetings was the problem of worldwide evil and its sources. The official record from the various sessions reported the following.

> We believe that we are engaged in constant spiritual warfare with the principalities and powers of evil, who are seeking to overthrow the Church and frustrate its task of world evangelization.[6]

> We affirm that spiritual warfare demands spiritual weapons, and that we must both preach the word in

the power of the Spirit, and pray constantly that we may enter into Christ's victory over the principalities and powers of evil.[7]

We agreed that evangelization is to bring people from darkness to light and from the power of Satan to God (Acts 26:17). This involves an inescapable element of spiritual warfare.[8]

In an official statement on its website, the Lausanne Council states:

Satan and "the rulers, authorities, the powers of this dark world, the spiritual forces of evil in the heavenly realms" are at work through:

Deceiving and distorting

Tempting to sin

Afflicting the body, emotions, mind, and will

Taking control of a person

Disordering of nature

Distorting the roles of social, economic, and political structures

Scapegoating as a means of legitimizing violence

Promoting self-interest, injustice, oppression, and abuse

The realm of the occult

False religions

All forms of opposition to God's work of salvation and the mission of the church

> ...Spiritual conflict involves more than one enemy;
> it must engage the flesh, the Devil and the world:
>
> > We view with alarm social evils such as injustice, poverty, ethnocentrism, racism, genocide, violence, environmental abuse, wars, as well as the violence, pornography, and occult in the media.
> >
> > These social evils are encouraged or supported by human institutions in which the principalities and powers work against God and his intention for humankind.
> >
> > The task of the Church in combating the principalities and powers in the socio-political context is to unmask their idolatrous pretensions, to identify their dehumanizing values and actions, and to work for the release of their victims. This work involves spiritual, political, and social actions.[9]

The delegates from many expressions of evangelicalism representing the worldwide body of Christ came to the corporate realization that principalities and powers in the heavenly realms were actively impeding the evangelization of the nations and were behind much of the distress and tragedy in human existence—a paradigm shift for many whose prior doctrine insisted on a defeated and impotent devil. Then came the hard part: What could be done about it?

The Lausanne Council goes on to say: "We call for discernment concerning magical uses of Christian terms and caution practitioners to avoid making spiritual conflict into Christian magic. Any suggestion that a particular technique or method in spiritual conflict ministry ensures success is a magical, sub-Christian understanding of God's workings....We warn against confusing correlations or coincidence with causation in reporting apparent victories as well as the uncritical use of undocumented accounts to establish the validity of cosmic warfare."[10]

The notes of the council also included a concern about the repercussions from the activities of some ministries that, while perhaps well intentioned, wreaked havoc by their flamboyant presumption in attempting to oust devils they did not know in territory where they had no authority.

"We were saddened by stories of people, emboldened by self-assured certainty and money, who come from outside and overwhelm local Christians and [sic] carrying out hit-and-run ministries of spiritual conflict 1) that presume superior knowledge of the local reality, 2) that treat local Christians as inferior or unaware, 3) that claim credit for things that local Christians have been praying and working toward for years, and 4) that leave uneven results and sometimes pain, alienation, and even persecution of the local church, while claiming great victory."[11]

In chapter 13 we will explore the meaning of "binding and loosing" in the context that what the church legislates on the earth, God confirms as legitimate in heaven. But it is important to consider here that after the Lausanne congress conferred legitimacy on the ministry of spiritual warfare, the cosmic battle intensified. Unfortunately the necessary protocol of war was not agreed upon or communicated by the council to every body that was represented. An acknowledgment of what *is* does not equate to an action plan of what to do next. Therefore each ministry did what was right in its own eyes.

Some ignored an inconvenient reality while others delved

headlong into calling out, casting down, decreeing, and declaring—sometimes creating an indistinguishable mix between spiritual presence and circus, leaving an unfortunate trail of disappointing results and a disillusioned body of believers. This is particularly true of the segment of the population sociologists call the Millennials, who do not perceive the organized church as capable of addressing the effects of evil in the world such as ethnic cleansing, extreme racism, poverty, plague, and violence.

In an article titled "The Rise of the Religious Left," Yale research fellow Claire Gordon writes, "Over a quarter of Millennials (those born after 1980), and 17% of the population overall, are religiously unaffiliated. The trend of 'believing without belonging' is sweeping the Western world, but in the US it is particularly striking; the number hovered at 7% through the 70s and 80s, and began its upward spiral in the 90s. Today, only 18% of young people attend church on a regular basis."[12]

This statistic should be sobering to church leadership. If the church is the only institution authorized by God to confront evil at its source, yet only 18 percent of its members are under thirty years of age, that suggests a crisis of confidence in current methods. Maybe we should try something else.

Chapter 10

SOMETHING WICKED THIS WAY COMES

C AN EVIL POWERS cause catastrophes in nature? The years 2010 and 2011 will be remembered for bringing global, devastating natural disasters.

In January 2010 an earthquake measuring 7.0 on the Richter scale shattered Haiti, one of the poorest island nations in the world, killing more than two hundred thousand people and leaving another 1.5 million homeless.[1] Many actively engaged in ministry perished as the quake made no distinction between the righteous and the unrighteous.

A pastor of a small church in Port Au Prince was in Florida to raise funds when the earthquake hit. He returned home to find his church destroyed with his wife and five children dead inside. Among those buried in the collapse of the Hotel Montana was a student from Lynn College serving on a mission trip. What we did not know at the time was that the devastation in Haiti would only be the beginning.

Barely one month later the largest earthquake in 2010 occurred in Chile in South America on February 27 when a devastating magnitude 8.8 left hundreds dead and more than 1.5 million people homeless.[2]

In February 2011, near Christchurch, New Zealand, a 6.3-magnitude earthquake struck the Canterbury region in New Zealand's South Island, killing 181 people and leaving thousands displaced.[3]

On March 11, 2011, the fifth-largest earthquake since 1900, registering 8.9, occurred off the coast of northern Japan, striking the northern coast and triggering a powerful tsunami followed by multiple aftershocks of 6.0 and above.[4] Devastating flooding followed, and a breach at a nuclear reactor created the possibility of the worst nuclear disaster of all time. Then came the nasty winds.

An extremely large and violent tornado outbreak, the largest in United States history, popularly known as the 2011 Super Outbreak, occurred April 25–28, 2011.[5] The eruption affected the Southern, Midwestern, and Northeastern United

States, leaving catastrophic destruction in its wake, especially across the state of Alabama. Destructive tornadoes affected Arkansas, Georgia, Mississippi, North Carolina, Tennessee, and Virginia, as well as several other areas throughout the Southern and Eastern United States.

A total of 336 tornadoes were confirmed in twenty-one states from Texas to New York, and there were even isolated tornadoes in Canada. Widespread and destructive twisters occurred on each day of the eruption, with April 27 being among the most prolific and destructive days in United States history. Four of the tornadoes were powerful enough to be rated EF5 on the Enhanced Fujita Scale, which is the highest ranking possible; typically there is only about one of these tornadoes in a given year. FEMA, the federally managed emergency response unit, was overwhelmed. Unbelievably, the disasters kept coming.[6]

On April 29, 2011, a strong tornado hit Tuscaloosa, Alabama, shattering the town's infrastructure and bringing the death toll to 337 people across the Southeast.[7] Next, shock and grief gripped Joplin, Missouri, on May 22, 2011, when it was struck by one of the deadliest twisters in nearly sixty years. Officials said the tornado was an EF5 with winds reaching two hundred miles an hour. In addition to the 132 people killed, more than 750 were hurt, making it the nation's deadliest tornado in more than six decades.[8]

Did God Do This?

If God did not cause this devastation, could He have prevented these disasters from happening? Do the sudden ravages of nature that maim, mutilate, and destroy the old and young, rich and poor, good and bad without distinction somehow advance the purposes of a supposed all-loving God?

Some Christian websites fired out messages that an angry God was sending warnings that the world must repent of its sin because the Rapture of the godly was near. Really? If it was God who brought about devastation to punish sin, why did He destroy the lives of the righteous alongside the unrighteous? Other minds insisted the catastrophes were natural phenomena, cyclical, and perhaps caused by external events such as global warming or the gravitational pull of the moon on the earth's tectonic plates.

Still others say the cause may be something else altogether because natural disaster is really natural evil. John Hick writes, "Natural evil is the evil that originates independently of human actions: in disease bacilli, earthquakes, storms, droughts, tornadoes, etc."[9]

In other words, environmental devastation may be evil, but it is nobody's fault. Neither God nor man has responsibility for the violence in weather, volcanoes, earthquakes, and so on. According to Old Testament accounts, God has sometimes used natural phenomena such as drought as a response to adversaries or to discipline people, but we cannot make a case that this is *always* or even *usually* the explanation for why nature behaves as it does.

If the violence done to the earth and people in 2010–2011 was a result of a naturally occurring pattern, the better question is why would an all-good and all-powerful God create such an inherently vicious and frightening natural scheme? Could it be that while God's wrath is not the instigator of catastrophe, the assumption that natural disaster is impersonal and therefore no one is to blame is wrong? Suppose the environmental system that governs the earth has itself fallen victim to morally responsible agents that have corrupted and warped its original design.

THE APPREHENSION OF NATURE

Boyd writes, "As the early church and almost every culture prior to modern Western culture has understood, it [nature] is subject to invisible agents who influence it for better or for worse.... Nature in its present state is not as the Creator created it to be, any more than humanity in its present state is as the Creator created it to be."[10]

Martin Luther is said to have taken seriously the psalmist's statement that the wind has wings. After a particularly severe and violent storm he is reported to have offered his opinions on the subject: "The devil provokes such storms, but good winds are produced by good angels. Winds are nothing but spirits, either good or evil. The devil sits there and snorts, and so do the angels when the winds are salubrious."[11]

Is it possible that lesser gods, interacting with human cooperatives, can bring about damage and desolation through natural phenomena to a region? Some respected Christian thinkers believe it is not only possible but also observable. Could such have been the case with the catastrophic events in Japan in 2011?

JAPAN'S RELIGIOUS HISTORY

Reflecting on the spiritual events he believes may have contributed to the tragedy in Japan, C. Peter Wagner writes, "Japan's culture has been virtually uninterrupted for 3,000 years. Paganism is deeply rooted in the warp and woof of the nation. The spirits over Japan have had their way, and they are not prepared to allow Christianity more than a token presence."[12]

Wagner recounts his participation with David Yonggi Cho of Korea in the mid-1980s to evangelize Japan in hopes of bringing 10 million people to Christ over the next decade. "However, it was not to be. Through the 1990s the rate of church growth in Japan remained unchanged and the year 2000 saw fewer than 1 million believers in the country—the same number as in 1990 and far short of the 10 million goal!"[13]

Admitting the lack of results despite all the spiritual resources poured into the country for more than a decade, Wagner reflected on the larger picture of Japan's religious history.

> The most serious setback for Japan's territorial spirits came during a seven-year period following World War II. Despite a Buddhist façade, Japan's most deeply entrenched spirits are the principalities controlling Shintoism, which is a spiritualized form of nationalism. The chief visible figure employed by these dark angels is the emperor. In the popular mind, the emperor was himself a deity. But as a part of the World War II peace process, Emperor Hirohito publicly denied this status and the Japanese government agreed to separate itself officially from any religious institution, including Shintoism.[14]

For more than thirty years Japan prospered and became an economic force in the world. Then in 1990 Hirohito died, and his son Akihito became the new emperor. Deciding to reverse his father's post–World War II position, Akihito made the controversial decision to include as part of his inauguration the ancient Daijo-sai ceremony, one in which the emperor is united to his imperial ancestress in such a manner as to share in a unique way in her divinity. Wikipedia describes the ritual.

> First, two special rice paddies are chosen and purified by elaborate Shinto purification rites...
>
> Meanwhile two thatched roof two-room huts are built within a corresponding special enclosure, using native Japanese building style which precedes all Chinese cultural influence. One room contains a large couch at its center...
>
> After a ritual bath the emperor is dressed entirely in the white silk dress of a Shinto priest, but with a special long train. Surrounded by courtiers, the emperor solemnly enters first the enclosure and then each of these huts in turn and performs the same ritual— from 6:30 to 9:30 PM in the first, and in the second from 12:30 to 3:30 AM.[15]

Wagner adds, "Notice that the only furniture in the second hut is a couch. The ceremony climaxes in a sexual encounter between the new emperor and the sun-goddess, Amaterasu Omikami, the chief spiritual ruler over the nation. It matters little whether the ensuing intercourse is physical (succubus) or spiritual. In the *invisible* world, the two ritually become one flesh and, through its supreme leader, the nation officially invites demonic control as long as he is emperor."[16]

Contrary to what his critics may say, Wagner is not indicting the Japanese people as responsible for the disasters that befell their country. He is merely presenting a witness of the religious history of the nation. If his interpretation is correct, the Japanese people may have been the victims of spiritual decisions in which they had no participation.

Those who are appalled at the link Wagner makes between the lesser gods and natural disaster argue that although aspects of nature may appear ugly when considered alone, when viewed from God's all-knowing point of view, they somehow contribute to the beauty of the whole. Not only is this argument repulsive to anyone who values human life in the slightest way, but it is also anathema to those who have experienced a nightmare.

After the earthquake in Haiti, American relief workers watched helplessly as hundreds of children endured the amputation of arms and legs without anesthesia to keep them from bleeding to death or dying from gangrene. Is the torturous suffering of human beings truly necessary to fulfill the greater plans of God? The notion that horrendous atrocities are reasonable collateral damage is hard to justify with the concept of an all-loving and all-powerful Creator. The sarcasm of Mark Twain in his version of the story of Noah's ark seems appropriate to such reasoning.

> The microbes were by far the most important part of the Ark's cargo, and the part the Creator was most anxious about and most infatuated with. They had to have good nourishment and pleasant accommodations. They were typhoid germs, and cholera germs, and hydrophobia germs, and lockjaw germs, and consumption germs, and black-plague germs, and some hundred of other aristocrats, specially precious creations,

golden bearers of God's love to man, blessed gifts of the infatuated father to His children.[17]

Even if the disobedience of Adam and Eve were the reason for the fall of mankind, it would not explain the destructive force of nature. They were given dominion over the earth to rule and subdue it, over the fish in the sea and the birds in the sky and over every living creature that moved on the ground. Scripture does not mention their mandate extending to tornadoes, earthquakes, volcanoes, tsunamis, hurricanes, ice storms, droughts, or floods; therefore, why would the consequences of their failure to execute their duties concerning the stewardship of the earth have repercussions for things outside of their defined responsibilities?

WHOSE FAULT IS IT?

I was managing the NBC affiliate in Minneapolis, Minnesota, when a devastating tornado tore through a small town in the fertile agricultural community near St. Peter. The day after, I was reviewing the rough footage from our news coverage where a little girl about six years old was being interviewed at the site of the worst destruction. She looked over the wreckage of her home and neighborhood when the reporter asked her what she was thinking. She put both hands on her little hips and looked him directly in the eye and demanded, "Whose fault is this? Who is going to clean up this mess?"

"The Maker and Framer of the World," wrote Athenagoras, "distributed and appointed...a multitude of angels and ministers...to occupy themselves about the elements, and the heavens, and the world, and the things in it, and the godly ordering of them all."[18]

But something went horribly wrong with the godly ordering part. Origen said that famines, scorching winds, and pestilence were not "natural" in God's creation at all but were rather the result of fallen angels bringing misery whenever and however they were able.[19]

If it is true that rebellious, high-ranking angels can manipulate the natural forces in the earth's atmosphere to bring destruction to innocent people, why does God not do something about it? The problem for God seems rooted in two immutable spiritual laws that He Himself has brought about. When these laws are linked together, what God *can* do in a specific situation is limited by what God *will* do according to the rules of conduct He established.

THE TENSION OF THE UNIVERSE

The immutable principles God has invoked are irrevocability and free will. As Romans 11:29 says, "God's gifts and his call are irrevocable." There are metaphysical constraints that God cannot avoid when He decides to limit Himself by giving other creatures free will. To the extent that God allows humans and angels to be self-determining, to that degree their moral choices must be irrevocable.

Jackson writes, "Although Satan became evil and God removed his authority through our risen Lord Jesus, He did not remove Satan's gifts. All gifts from God are irrevocable. For example, many rock groups today are formed by former church members who sang in the choir and led worship. Though they have fallen in their relationship with God,

He has not removed their gift of music that was originally intended for worship."[20] God has prevented Himself from removing a gift because of its misuse. He gives it unconditionally and without limitation, scope, or duration.

An objection to this line of reasoning arises out of Colossians 2:14: "Having canceled the written code, with its regulations, that was against us and that stood opposed to us; he took it away, nailing it to the cross. And having disarmed the powers and authorities, he made a public spectacle of them, triumphing over them by the cross."

Does this scripture mean that the lesser gods that held mankind in captivity lost their power to do further damage? Peter T. O'Brien, head of the New Testament Department of Moore Theological College in New South Wales, Australia, explains it like this. "He [Jesus] is the 'head' over all the principalities and powers for God has divested them of all authority in him (2:13). Although they continue to exist, inimical to man and his interests (cf. Rom. 8:38, 39) their final defeat is inevitable."[21]

C. Peter Wagner writes in *Warfare Prayer*, "On the cross Jesus disarmed principalities and powers assuring Satan's ultimate defeat. But while Satan is defeated, he is not yet destroyed. Even after Jesus's death and resurrection, Paul refers to Satan as 'the god of this age' (2 Cor. 4:4) and the 'prince of the power of the air' (Eph. 2:22). John says that 'the whole world is under the sway of the wicked one' (1 John 5:19). Both Paul and John were aware that Jesus will ultimately be the ruler of our cities. But their language indicate that they also knew that the degree to which the will of God is materialized in our cities and in our daily lives in the present age depends a great deal on how we human beings, through the power that God has delegated to us by His Holy Spirit, successfully confront and neutralize the prince of the power of the air."[22]

(It should be noted that Wagner differs with Payne and Jackson and believes it is within the purview of believers to confront territorial demons directly. His arguments are detailed in his book *Warfare Prayer*.)

While God can at any time and occasionally does interrupt the laws He has set in place to govern the world, generally He does not. Law is impersonal. It works the same way for all people all the time. The law of gravity applies to those who understand it exists and to those who do not. A righteous person who falls from a tall building will hit the ground with the same force and consequences as one who is unrighteous.

God established spiritual laws as well as natural ones to govern the cosmos. Those laws include enduing self-determining, moral agents with power and authority, whether they are angelic or human, to affect how things are. He is a God of order, not chaos. He limits Himself to the arrangement He has established. Therefore, when rebellious lesser gods abuse their powers and bring about environmental disaster, in most cases He does *not* do what He *could* do.

ARE HUMAN BEINGS HELPLESS AGAINST EVIL ANGELIC POWERS?

Let me be clear about one thing: the earthbound occult, carnal, and menacing spirits Jesus dealt with in the Gospels and authorized us to also confront are not the same as the cosmic-level evil angelic powers. The latter, for the most part, are at war with God over the fates of nations, not the fate of individuals. So while we can take authority over a spirit of depression, for instance, commanding "Baal" is an entirely different matter. Attempting to command a high-ranking evil angelic being is, in fact, quite dangerous.

There are clear and present dangers in pulling on the tail of Leviathan. Flesh and blood are not a match against powerful, supernatural beings that are not encumbered by the need to eat, drink, and breathe, and who do not bleed, die, or experience pain. Perhaps that is why Psalm 91:11 says God gives His angels charge over us, to protect us against the attacks of demonic powers against whom we are ill-equipped to resist.

While some insist that being filled with the Holy Spirit gives us the authority and ability to combat and dethrone supernatural entities, there is considerable disagreement among scholars and theologians as to whether this is true. What does the New Testament say the work of the Holy Spirit is?

- He empowers God's purposes through people (Matt. 1:18; 3:11).

- People are baptized in His name (Matt. 28:19).

- He is not to be blasphemed against (Mark 3:29).

- He speaks through people (Mark 13:11).

- He reveals the future (Luke 2:26).

- He empowers us to stand against Satan (Luke 4:1).

- He teaches us what we need to know and what to say (John 14:26).

- He enables us to be witnesses (Acts 1:8).

- He enables us to speak in other tongues (Acts 2:4).

- He enables preaching (Acts 4:31).

- He encourages (Acts 9:31).

- He summons people for specific purpose (Acts 13:2).

- He directs our path (Acts 13:4).

- He prevents us from certain paths (Acts 16:6).

- He warns us of impending danger (Acts 21:11).

- He sanctifies (Rom. 15:16).

- He marks us with a seal (Eph. 1:13).

- He can be grieved (Eph. 4:30).

- He convicts (1 Thess. 1:5).

- He conveys gifts (Heb. 2:4).

What we do not see listed among the works of the Holy Spirit is direct engagement against supernatural evil powers to prevent devastating natural disasters where thousands of human lives are at risk. Although Jesus rebuked a storm, He did not instruct anyone else to try it. The Holy Spirit does the work He has been given to do. Jesus said He had finished the work the Father gave Him to do (John 17:4).

If there is yet an advocate who can legally intervene between the people of the earth and the ravages of rebellious celestial beings intent upon our destruction, it must be someone else's job. The defense of the earth and its people against an onslaught of evil lies with the holy angels who did not rebel and who remain faithful servants of God to protect and provide for the needs of humanity. Their duties have been outlined in an online commentary by theologian John Bechtle, DMin:[23]

- Revealing: They serve as messengers to communicate God's will to men. They helped reveal the law to Moses (Acts 7:52–53) and served as the carriers of much of the material in Daniel and Revelation.

- Guiding: Angels gave instructions to Joseph about the birth of Jesus (Matt. 1–2), to the women at the tomb, to Philip (Acts 8:26), and to Cornelius (Acts 10:1–8).

- Providing: God has used angels to provide physical needs such as food for Hagar (Gen. 21:17–20), Elijah (1 Kings 19:6), and Christ after His temptation (Matt. 4:11).

- Protecting: Keeping God's people out of physical danger, as in the cases of Daniel and the lions and his three friends in the fiery furnace (Dan. 6; 3).

- Delivering: Getting God's people out of danger once they're in it. Angels released the apostles from prison in Acts 5 and repeated the process for Peter in Acts 12.

- Strengthening and encouraging: Angels strengthened Jesus after His temptation (Matt. 4:11), encouraged the apostles to keep preaching after releasing them from prison (Acts 5:19–20), and told Paul that everyone on his ship would survive the impending shipwreck (Acts 27:23–25).

- Answering prayer: God often uses angels as His means of answering the prayers of His people (Dan. 9:20–24; 10:10–12; Acts 12:1–17).

- Caring for believers at the moment of death: In the story of Lazarus and the rich man, we read that angels carried the spirit of Lazarus to "Abraham's bosom" when he died (Luke 16:22).

When Lucifer rebelled in heaven, it was Michael—not Yahweh and not Adonai—who battled against him and cast him down to the earth. When the prince of Persia prevented an angel from reaching Daniel, it was Michael who overpowered the prince to secure the angel's release. Why? Because a hallmark of God's kingdom is restraint and justice: "eye for eye, tooth for tooth, hand for hand, foot for foot, burn for burn, wound for wound, bruise for bruise" (Exod. 21:24–25, NAS). There is no equitableness in the unleashed wrath of Omnipotence against a created being.

God established a hierarchy of heavenly host for a reason. The Catholic Encyclopedia describes the ranking. "We know on the authority of Scripture that there are nine orders of angels, viz., Angels, Archangels, Virtues, Powers, Principalities, Dominations, Throne, Cherubim and Seraphim. That there are Angels and Archangels nearly every page of the Bible tells us, and the books of the Prophets talk of Cherubim and Seraphim. St. Paul, too, writing to the Ephesians enumerates four orders when he says: 'above all Principality, and Power, and Virtue, and Domination'; and again, writing to the Colossians he says: 'whether Thrones, or Dominations, or Principalities, or Powers.' If we now join these two lists together we have five Orders, and adding Angels and Archangels, Cherubim and Seraphim, we find nine Orders of Angels."[24]

Scripture supports that when there is disobedience within the angelic realm, it is addressed by another angel of equal or higher rank who is loyal to God. When evil lesser gods unleash their powers against a nation, individuals, or people groups, the order to stand down must come from a higher-ranking celestial authority.

The evidence is undeniable that flesh and blood unaided is unlikely to survive an unrestrained frontal attack from a super-natural power intent on its destruction. The key word in the previous sentence is *unaided*. Perhaps we have been praying the whirlwind in our attempts to bind, decree, and direct hurricanes, tornadoes, and earthquakes, over which humans have no authority, when we should have been asking God to release the angels of Revelation on behalf of the people in harm's way.

> After this I saw four angels standing at the four corners of the earth, holding back the four winds of the earth to prevent any wind from blowing on the land or on the sea or on any tree. Then I saw another angel coming up from the east, having the seal of the living God. He called out in a loud voice to the four angels who had been given power to harm the land and the sea: "Do not harm the land or the sea or the trees until we put a seal on the foreheads of the servants of our God."
>
> —Revelation 7:1–3

Perhaps we would be more effective in our prayers to mitigate the ravages of environmental calamity if we recognized the authority we have to govern the earth does not extend to the forces of nature. Should we not rather ask God to set the celestial cavalry against evil gods that have hijacked the forces of weather and sea for the purpose of destruction?

Chapter 11

A SLIPPERY SLOPE—A WORD OF CAUTION

WHATEVER ELSE THEY may do in the cosmos, angels on the earth serve the purposes of God for the well-being of humanity. Jesus spoke of little ones having an angel assigned to them (Matt. 18:10). The idea of a personal guardian angel is deeply rooted in the spiritual psyche of many people of different faiths. We have already seen several examples in both Testaments of angels penetrating the thin veil that separates this reality from the heavenly realms to interact with human beings at times of crisis.

This was true even of Jesus. Mark 1:13 tells us that angels were sent to Him in the desert to minister to His needs after His encounter with Satan. In modern times the testimonies of people who have had encounters with visible angels, while not all credible, are still too many to dismiss. A fascinating story is told about the prophet Elisha and his servant, who found themselves penned down and surrounded by an army set to kill them.

> When the servant of the man of God got up and went out early the next morning, an army with horses and chariots had surrounded the city. "Oh, my lord, what shall we do?" the servant asked.
>
> "Don't be afraid," the prophet answered. "Those who are with us are more than those who are with them."
>
> And Elisha prayed, "O Lord, open his eyes so he may see." Then the Lord opened the servant's eyes, and he looked and saw the hills full of horses and chariots of fire all around Elisha.
>
> As the enemy came down toward him, Elisha prayed to the Lord, "Strike these people with blindness." So he struck them with blindness, as Elisha had asked.
>
> —2 Kings 6:15–18

This is one of the earliest depictions of the heavenly host as a warring army prepared to intervene in a human battle. It should be noted that although Elisha saw them and knew they were there for his benefit, he did not order them to do anything. He prayed to the Lord.

In some circles in recent years there has been a popular, but I believe deeply flawed, teaching that angels are all about us waiting for a person to give them orders to do something. God commands angels; people do not. When Jesus was arrested, Peter lashed out at a guard to prevent His capture. Jesus rebuked Peter, saying, "Do you think I cannot call on my Father, and he will at once put at my disposal more than twelve legions of angels?" (Matt. 26:53). Even Jesus did not presume to summon angels while confined to His human nature.

There are many reports in the Bible describing face-to-face encounters between people and supernatural beings. In not a single one is there anything less than fear and awe experienced on the part of the people, most of whom bowed down in submission. Except for a call to praise God in Psalm 148, there is only one recorded instance where a man attempted to give orders to an angel. For all the romance Western interpreters seem to assign to the story, it turned out to be a painful and arguably foolish thing to do.

Jacob tried wrestling with an angel to secure his blessing, ended up crippled in his hip, and walked with a severe limp the rest of his life (Gen. 32:25). In another account Zechariah presumed only to question whether Gabriel was telling him the truth and was struck dumb until his son, John the Baptist, was born (Luke 1:18–20).

If there are legions of angels waiting to intervene for us when we are in trouble, how do we get them to do so? Clearly the evidence indicates it is not a given that they will. Since they are God's servants and not ours, our only recourse is to ask God to engage them in battle—*real* battle, the outcome of which is, therefore, not certain.

But why should that be necessary? Will God not act on behalf of the righteous regardless of whether or not He is asked to do so? Sometimes He does, and sometimes He simply does not. No one can answer why. But if Jesus, knowing God's perfect plan, had to pray in order for His Father's will to be accomplished on earth, how much more do the rest of us have to pray?

Boyd writes:

> The view that the purpose of prayer is not to change God or change things but only to change *us* is pious-sounding teaching many evangelical Christians instinctively accept as true. This is, after all, the only understanding of prayer that is logically compatible with the Augustinian understanding of God as omni-determinative, impassible, and altogether timeless. The only trouble with it is that it is altogether unscriptural.
>
> The primary purpose of prayer, as illustrated throughout Scripture, is precisely to change the way things are. Crucial matters, including much of God's own activity, are contingent upon our prayer....In the same way that a person's deliverance from a poten-tial rapist may completely hang upon whether others heed her call and respond, so too events in the spiri-tual realm seem at times genuinely contingent upon what others do or do not do.[1]

If God would or could always do what He wants to do in the first place without needing to be asked, Jesus's instruc-tions to us in Matthew 9:37–38 to ask the Lord of the harvest to send workers into the field would be meaningless. In 2 Chronicles 7:14 God says that the people who are called by His name must humble themselves and pray; *then* He will hear and heal the land, implying that if they do not pray, He may not hear or heal. Words from Ezekiel are particularly sobering:

> I looked for a man among them who would build up the wall and stand before me in the gap on behalf of the land so I would not have to destroy it, but I found none. So I will pour out my wrath on them and consume them with my fiery anger, bringing down on their own heads all they have done, declares the Sovereign LORD.
>
> —EZEKIEL 22:30–31

It is not clear from Scripture whether we are to petition God to send angels to assist us in the same way we might petition Him to send anyone else to our rescue, but neither is it expressly prohibited. What is forbidden is the *worship* of angels. What is clear is that human interaction with angels can prove to be a very slippery slope.

THE HERESY AT COLOSSAE

Colossae was an important city of Phrygia in Asia Minor, east of Ephesus. While it is not known that Paul ever visited the city, he became concerned of the reports that a serious distortion of the gospel had arisen among the believers. The heresy combined philosophical speculations, astral powers, reverence of angelic intermediaries, food taboos, and ascetic practices influenced by Judaism. Paul warned that the believers were in danger of being taken captive to a philosophy and deception that included the worship of angels (Col. 2:8–18).

The proclivity of humans to seek favor and protection through angels is abundant in the history of many religions. The fact that God Himself has on occasion authorized angels to interact with humans as messengers and guides diminishes some of the natural apprehension a person might otherwise have about connecting personally with the supernatural. As we have already seen, once people become comfortable that angels may protect or rescue them from difficulty, it can be a short leap to begging them to do so in exchange for worship.

The holy angels who remain loyal to Yahweh are quick to reject the attempts of humans to worship them, as demonstrated in Revelation when the writer John says he fell down at the angel's feet to worship him. The angel replied, "Do not do it! I am a fellow servant with you and with your brothers who hold to the testimony of Jesus" (Rev. 19:10).

The balance beam between recognition that angels remain active in the affairs of the earth and inadvertently slipping into a prohibited relationship with them is often a delicate one for well-intentioned people to navigate. For example, there are recognized, albeit controversial, sub-sects of the church who are adherents to orthodoxy, but who also see themselves as having a sacred ministry as intermediaries to petition the assistance of angels. Perhaps the most well known is Opus Sanctorum Angelorum.

Opus Sanctorum Angelorum

Opus Sanctorum Angelorum, or "Work of the Holy Angels," is a public Roman Catholic association, in conformity with traditional doctrine and with the directive of the Holy See, that promotes devotion to angels. It spreads devotion to the holy angels among the faithful, exhorts them to pray for priests, and promotes love for Christ in His passion and union with it. It is active particularly in Austria, where it originated, and in Germany, but also in Portugal, Brazil, Mexico, India, the Philippines, Italy, and the United States. The association was founded in 1949 by a group of priests and seminarians in Innsbruck, Austria, to seek the aid of the angels in support of the church and the priesthood and for the salvation of souls.[2]

The association drew inspiration from the accounts that Gabriele Bitterlich gave of her private revelations. She claimed to have received visions of the angels, including their names and their functions. When it became widely known that some of her followers were circulating sensational and controversial theories of spiritual warfare between angels and demons, Cardinal Joseph Höffner, Archbishop of Cologne, asked the Holy See to institute an inquiry on December 1, 1977. The Congregation for the Doctrine of the Faith carried out the requested investigation and responded on September 24, 1983, with a letter, known by its incipit, *Litteris diei*, that laid down the following guidelines.

> 1. In fostering devotion to the Holy Angels,
>   Opus Angelorum must follow the doctrine of
>   the church. In particular, its members were
>   not to use the "names" of angels derived from
>   the alleged private revelation attributed to Mrs.
>   Gabriele Bitterlich, nor use those names in any
>   teaching or prayers of the community.[3]

2. Opus Angelorum is not to demand or even propose to its members what is called the Promise of Secrecy, although with regard to the internal affairs of the Opus Angelorum, it is lawful to maintain the discretion that befits members of the church's institutes.[4]

3. The Opus Angelorum will strictly observe the norms of the liturgy, especially regarding the Eucharist.[5]

This was followed up by a decree of June 6, 1992, which repeated the contents of the 1983 letter and, in view of incorrect interpretation and application of that letter, laid down the following rules:

1. The theories arising from the revelations alleged to have been received by Mrs. Gabriele Bitterlich about the world of the Angels, their personal names, their groupings and functions, can neither be taught, nor made use of in any way—explicitly or implicitly—in the organization and working structure (*Baugerust*) of "Opus Angelorum", as well as in worship, prayers, spiritual formation, public and private spirituality, in ministry and the apostolate. The same provision applies to any other Institute or Association recognized by the Church. The use and dissemination of books or the writings containing the aforementioned theories, either inside or outside the Association, is forbidden.

2. The various forms of Consecration to the Angels (*Engelweihen*) practiced in "Opus Angelorum" are prohibited.

3. In addition, the so-called remote administration

of the Sacraments (*Fernspendung*) is prohibited, as well as the insertion of prayers or rituals which, directly or indirectly, refer to these theories into the Eucharistic Liturgy or the Liturgy of the Hours.

4. Exorcisms may be practized only according to the Church Norms and Discipline in this regard, with the Formulas She has approved.

5. A Delegate with special faculties, appointed by the Holy See, will verify and insist, in consultation with the Bishops, on the application of the Norms laid down above. He will see to it that the relations between "Opus Angelorum" and the Order of Canons Regular of the Holy Cross are clarified and regularized.[6]

The delegate chosen was the Dominican priest Father Benoit Duroux, who handed over this function to another Dominican priest, Father Daniel Ols, in March 2010.[7] Yet under the November 5, 2010, banner headline "Vatican Warns Bishops on Angel-Worshipping Sect," bishops around the world were warned to monitor the Opus Angelorum sect.

The article stated that the sect's founder, Gabriele Bitterlich, "became obsessed with angels and wrote extensively about their fight against demons." Her teaching included the beliefs that "women who suffered a miscarriage had been attacked by demons, and that journalists and communists were held in special regard by these evil spirits." Certain animals were most susceptible to demonic possession: "most grey, spotted and black cats, pigs, smooth haired dogs, flies and rats." According to Bitterlich, "the faithful could only protect themselves from these demons by worshipping angels." The article went on to state that after conducting two reports, Catholic theologian

Johann Auer said he believed Bitterlich's views were a result of "paranoid schizophrenia."[8]

Cardinal Levada, the Prefect of the Congregation for the Doctrine of the Faith, issued a letter stating that some priests who left Opus Angelorum were seeking to "restore what, according to them, would be the 'authentic Opus Angelorum,' that is, a movement which professes and practices all those things which were forbidden."[9] Levada's letter said "very discrete propaganda in favour of this wayward movement, which is outside of any ecclesiastical control, is taking place, aimed at presenting it as if it were in full communion with the Catholic Church," and he called on bishops to be watchful of disruptive activities and to ban any they identify.[10]

What does Opus Angelorum say about itself? The following comes from the official Opus Sanctorum Angelorum website.

> The distinctiveness of the association Opus Sanctorum Angelorum consists in the fact that its members take the devotion to the holy angels to its full development which is manifested and made concrete by a "consecration to the Holy Angels", as is similarly the case in the history of the Church with regard to the devotion to the Sacred Heart of Jesus and to the Immaculate Heart of Mary (consecration to the Heart of Jesus and to the Immaculate Heart of his Mother).
>
> Through the consecration to the Guardian Angel one enters into the Work of the Holy Angels. The consecration to the Holy Angels is made by those members who want to do more in the pursuit of the spiritual goals of the movement. This consecration is understood as a covenant of the faithful with the holy angels, that is, as a conscious and explicit act of

acknowledging and taking seriously their mission and place in the economy of salvation. Just as many spiritualities have their typical expressions, as for example the *"Totus tuus"* of Pope John Paul II, so also the spirituality of the consecration to the Holy Angels in the *Opus Angelorum* could be characterized by the words *"cum sanctis angelis"*, that is, *"with the holy angels"* or *"in communion with the holy angels"*.

In fact, by faith and the theological virtue of charity, it is possible for the faithful to "live together" with the holy angels as true friends, and thus also is made possible an intimate spiritual collaboration with them for the goals of God's plan of salvation in relation to all creatures, especially since on the part of the angels their cooperation in all our good works is guaranteed.

This living together and spiritual collaboration of the faithful with the holy angels, in which consists, according to the above-mentioned statues, the proper "nature" of the *Opus Angelorum*, obviously demands not only faith in and a love for the holy angels—and in the first place for one's own Guardian Angel—but also the prudent application of the criteria for the "discernment of spirits".[11]

BE CAREFUL WHAT YOU WHISTLE FOR

My brother is one of the last of the real cowboys. He is a rugged individualist who lives in a house built in the shape of the state of Texas in an isolated section of the hill country north of San Antonio. Tony is a commonsense, no-nonsense frontiersman who, by his own admission, has "been in a scrape or two." The solitude portions of his life have caused him to instinctively and experientially understand more about the dance between the natural and supernatural than academics can ever learn through scholarship alone.

He tells the story of being on a hunting trip in the west with a *compadre* named Jesse. While sitting around the campfire in the deep darkness of a landscape where electricity had not yet come, Jesse pulled a whistle-like contraption from his vest pocket.

"Watch this," he said as he raised it to his lips and began to blow.

An eerie, ear-piercing squeal came forth. Tony grabbed it out of his hand and demanded to know what it was.

"Sounds just like a rabbit caught in a trap, doesn't it?" Jesse answered. "It's for calling wolves."

Tony threw the device into the campfire. "Idiot!" he said as the distant howls of creatures of the night began to move closer. "Don't you know that what you whistle for will come?"

Prayer is like a whistle. That which we summon will eventually come. Adages become such because they are true. "Be careful what you pray for; you might get it" is a good illustration. "Pray that you will not fall into temptation," Jesus said in Luke 22:40. Temptation is where we find ourselves when we are scared and desperate and God seems unresponsive. If God will not answer, perhaps someone else will.

"Call up for me the spirit of Samuel," Saul told the witch at Endor. (See 1 Samuel 28:11.) I have heard many teachings on this passage of Scripture over the years. All of them centered on the prohibition against consulting with spiritists or mediums. While this is wise counsel, unfortunately, it misses the greater point altogether. Samuel actually came.

Chapter 12

CAN FALLEN ANGELS BE REDEEMED?

A SHORT SEARCH ON the Internet will disclose hundreds of Christian websites that offer an absolute answer to the question of whether fallen angels can be redeemed. One need not spend time going past the first page of a Google search because all sites give the same response: no, unequivocally, there is no redemption for rebellious angels. Apart from the good news of Jesus, it is hard to find another topic on the

Internet about which there is such uniformity and assuredness among Christian organizations.

One will find there is considerable disagreement about baptism, speaking in tongues, ordination of women, gifts of the Spirit, divorce, homosexuality, tattoos, who goes to heaven, and whether hell exists. But concerning the question of redemption for angels, among conventional Christianity there is no debate, no discussion, no what-ifs. Unanimity, however, does not mean infallibility. Fewer than two centuries ago most Christian organizations also agreed that the acceptability of slavery was clearly supported in the Bible.

A neutral person who has not been indoctrinated by Sunday school lessons might observe that the evidence for the certainty of the Christian response about the fate of angels is not founded in certainty at all, but it is based on what the Bible does not say rather than what it does.

The prevailing narrative is that because the angels had perfect knowledge and access to God, they were without excuse for their disobedience, whereas mankind was deceived by Satan. Therefore, redemption for the sin of man, which history chronicles to have been as egregious as any attributed to celestial beings, is provided for because man did not have the full revelation of God, as did the angels. Whether or not this is a correct answer, it cannot possibly be known for certain and is not proved by any known documents of the Old or New Testaments.

Genesis 1:26 says mankind was created in the mirrorlike image of God. We have no such definitive testimony as to what angels were created to be like, but it seems difficult to imagine a higher standard. Nor do we know when they were created or what their relationship to Yahweh was except that they were worshippers of His glory and executors of His will on the earth. We do not know at what point in history Lucifer rebelled or the circumstances that led to other angels being united with him against God.

Revelation 12:9 is the only verse that refers to one-third of the heavenly host being cast down with Lucifer, but we do not know the circumstances surrounding this event. We do not know if the angels fell into condemnation at the same time as Lucifer, but it seems unlikely. If the accounts of Ezekiel 28 and Isaiah 14 are about the rogue archangel, both passages fail to mention that there were any other heavenly beings involved.

Some Jewish commentaries and other writings, such as the testimony of Enoch, support the belief that the fall of the angels occurred when the sons of God went down to the daughters of men and copulated with them. While we have speculated in this book that the desire for worship from humanity may have been the reason the angels overstepped their boundaries, we do not know from where or from whom they got the idea. For example, Adam and Eve did not think to question or second-guess the plans of God until Satan raised suspicion about God's motives. How can we be sure something similar did not occur with the angels?

If Lucifer could cast doubt on God's trustworthiness in the minds of creatures made in His exact likeness, is it so far-fetched to think such a talented deceiver might not have been able to do the same thing with other angels? We simply cannot know for sure.

What we can know is there are verses in the Bible that we are challenged to definitively explain.

> For God was pleased to have all his fullness dwell in him, and through him to reconcile to himself all things, whether things on earth or things in heaven, by making peace through his blood, shed on the cross.
>
> —COLOSSIANS 1:19–20

What are the things in heaven in need of reconciliation? If this verse is not referring to the rebellious angels, what does it mean? Verse 23 goes on to say:

> This is the gospel that you heard and that has been proclaimed to every creature under heaven, and of which I, Paul, have become a servant.

What creatures under heaven is Paul talking about? If the good news was meant only for human beings, why did he not say so? In writing to the Romans, Paul presents a provocative declaration of the power of redemption.

> For the anxious longing of the creation waits eagerly for the revealing of the *sons of God*. For the creation was subjected to futility, not willingly, but because of Him who subjected it, in hope that the creation itself also will be set free from its slavery to corruption into the freedom of the glory of the children of God.
>
> —ROMANS 8:19–21, NAS, EMPHASIS ADDED

Who are the sons of God the creation is waiting to see revealed? Does this mean human beings? Maybe, but not definitively. In the Old Testament the phrase "sons of God" was used eight times to refer to the angels. Adam Clarke's commentary on these verses reads: "There is considerable difficulty in this and the four following verses: and the difficulty lies chiefly in the meaning of the word *hee* (NT:3588) *ktisis* (NT:2937), which we translate the creature, and creation. Some think that by it the brute creation is meant; others apply it to the Jewish people; others to the godly; others to the Gentiles; others to the good angels; and others to the fallen spirits, both angelic and human. Dissertations without end have been written on it; and it does not appear that the Christidal world are come to any general agreement on the subject."[1]

Without question, the punishment for the rebellion of the angels was severe.

> For if God did not spare angels when they sinned, but sent them to hell, putting them into gloomy dungeons to be held for judgment...if he condemned the cities of Sodom and Gomorrah by burning them to ashes, and made them an example of what is going to happen to the ungodly...
>
> —2 PETER 2:4, 6

What does it mean to be held for judgment? When a person has been charged with a crime, he or she is usually placed in jail awaiting trial and sentencing by a judge. Even if the person has been found to be guilty, it can never be a foregone conclusion what kind of sentence the judge might impose. He might render the most severe punishment allowable by law, he may impose leniency and probation, or he might agree that the sentence will be mitigated by time served.

In the same verses that describe the angels being held in gloomy dungeons for judgment, there is a reference to what happened to Sodom and Gomorrah. The biblical account tells us the cities were destroyed, and according to Jeremiah 50:40, no one would ever live again. But in Ezekiel we find the Lord saying something else.

> However, I will restore the fortunes of Sodom and her daughters and of Samaria and her daughters, and your fortunes along with them.
>
> —Ezekiel 16:53

The ultimate fate of Sodom becomes even more confusing because of something Jesus said when speaking about the future judgment of towns that failed to extend hospitality to the disciples should they visit.

> I tell you the truth, it will be more bearable for Sodom and Gomorrah on the day of judgment than for that town.
>
> —Matthew 10:15

This should give us pause at several levels. Jesus has exalted the sin of selfishness and bad manners to be more deserving of greater punishment than that of Sodom and Gomorrah. Also implied is that whatever the ultimate judgment of the angels associated with the two cities might be, it appears to be undecided.

Whether there can be a plan of redemption for fallen angels in God's design and intent to reconcile all things to Himself rests in His sovereignty. His history has been one of a God in resolute pursuit of His errant creation. The question theologians, who are comfortable in their certainty that "things in heaven (fallen angels)" cannot be redeemed, must wrestle with is how to explain what Paul meant in Colossians 1:20, which declares that the blood of Jesus is truly sufficient to cover all sins for all time for all creation, both things in heaven and on the earth.

A DIFFERENT GOSPEL

Galatia was a Roman province that included Lycania, Isauria, Prygia, and Pisidia. It is now in southern Turkey. The purpose of Paul's epistle to the young church was to eradicate the doctrinal errors that had been recently introduced by hostile Judaizers and to urge the Galatian Christians to hold firmly to what Paul had taught them at the beginning. From Paul's letter we understand the people to have been generally impressionable, somewhat fickle, and even quick-tempered. Paul was concerned that Judaistic teachers had subverted his work by teaching a new type of legalism.

> But even if we or an angel from heaven should preach a gospel other than the one we preached to you, let him be eternally condemned! As we have already said, so now I say again: If anybody is preaching to you a gospel other than what you accepted, let him be eternally condemned!
>
> —GALATIANS 1:8–9

In Matthew 13:52 Jesus said that every teacher who has been instructed in the ways of the kingdom will bring out of the storehouse of the knowledge of God new revelation to complement the old. Jesus also said that our paradigms— our mind-sets—must not be like old wineskins that would rip apart from the energy and expansion of the new wine. The challenge for all seekers of God from all time has been to separate revelation from vain imagination. Even among the sects of Judaism there were vast differences in what was believed about God and the supernatural. The Pharisees believed in angels, demons, judgment, miracles, a God who intervenes in the affairs of the world, and the end of the age. The Sadducees believed in none of these things.

Among the many doctrines of modern churches who all believe in the same God are many interpretations of what are called the nonessentials. Most hold a united belief in the virgin birth; the life, death, and resurrection of Jesus; His sacrifice as the efficacy to address the problem of sin; and the ultimate reconciliation of all things to God the Father.

As long as history continues, we should expect new revelation and understanding to come as to how we comprehend the Word of God in a changing world setting. While the Scriptures do not change, how we understand their application must. Otherwise it is not a "living" word at all. Living things evolve. The challenge for believers is to discern between ideas that are new revelation from the Holy Spirit versus what may well represent "a different gospel." Case in point, the Covenant of One Heaven.

Pactum De Singularis Caelum

The Society of One Heaven is a self-proclaimed free society of united men, women, and higher-order spirits, living and deceased, formed by sacred covenant. It was founded in 2009 under the direction of Frank O'Collins. The central idea underpinning One Heaven is that "'you cannot have peace on Earth until you have peace in Heaven'—in other words, until a legitimate, respected document exists as proof that the war in heaven is over and that all major religions see their central beliefs fulfilled, there can be no peace or guarantee of the future prosperity and survival of the Homo Sapien [*sic*] species."[2]

The pact represents a complex, detailed, and cumbersome manifesto combining teachings from many of the world's religions with considerable speculation about the interaction of the supernatural and natural realms. One article of the pact concerns the war in heaven under the subheading "Peace in Heaven, peace on Earth":

> That there is peace both in Heaven on Earth, now and forever. So as above, so it is below. For peace to exist on Earth, peace and unity must reign in Heaven. So long as Hell exists, Heaven is at war. Therefore, for peace to exist in Heaven, this document exists to proclaim the end of the war in Heaven, the unification of Heaven and the end of Hell. By the official end of Hell, Heaven can be united in peace. Therefore, the Earth may also be united in peace to the proposition that we are all ultimately higher order beings who collectively believe in a common life after death in the framework of One united Heaven.[3]

SEEKER BEWARE

The idea of peace in heaven and on earth is the aim of those who believe that the kingdom of God should be advancing until the kingdoms of this world (however *world* might be defined) become the kingdoms of our God, as Revelation 11:15 declares. Yet there are spiritual boundaries that we should not cross. The Society of One Heaven represents an extraordinary distortion of the reconciliation of all things in heaven and on earth as Colossians 1:19–20 declares. As we have seen in an earlier chapter, there exist places between the realms of reality where the veil is thin. Some people both alive and dead, angels, and demons are known to have penetrated the veil and interacted with the inhabitants on the other side. A stern warning against this practice is found in the Old Testament.

> There shall not be found among you anyone who makes his son or his daughter pass through the fire, one who uses divination, one who practices witchcraft, or one who interprets omens, or a sorcerer, or one who casts a spell, or a medium, or a spiritist, or one who calls up the dead.
>
> —DEUTERONOMY 18:10–11, NAS

The Greek word for "sorcerer" means swindler. Perhaps part of Yahweh's prohibition to the Jews from engaging in these practices was to protect them from being manipulated through witchcraft or robbed through charlatans.

The dominion mandate given to mankind over the earth does not extend to the parallel universes of heaven, hell, Hades, paradise, and whoever might reside therein. The idea that humans and other powers should somehow unite to seize the government of the cosmos and write a constitution declaring peace on earth and heaven and the destruction of hell does not have its origins in anything revealed in Scripture.

While the claims of the Covenant of One Heaven are outrageous to most Christians, let me suggest that some within orthodoxy would consider them no more so than the idea promoted by proponents of cosmic level spiritual warfare that human beings can thwart, cast down, or do anything at all to a celestial power. If one could somehow capture or cast down lesser gods, it is not such a broad leap to suppose he might also be able to broker a truce with them.

Bad ideas pay compound interest. It is a bad idea of the worst kind for human beings to insert themselves into the unresolved fray between God and His angels.

Chapter 13

YOU WILL HAVE WHAT YOU SAY

EVIL FLOURISHES IN poverty and wealth, ignorance and knowledge, superstition and secularism. It manifests in greed, lust, bigotry, racism, idolatry, fear, violence, and rabid religious certainty. It is not based in logic and therefore cannot be reasoned with. It is opportunistic and scheming. At the end of all its descriptors, evil emanates from a league of powerful, supernatural beings that crave, ravish, ravage, and ultimately attempt to devour human prey. The fallen angels who are organized under Satan lust for the flesh and worship of all mankind. Satan himself was interested in only three: Job, Adam, and Jesus of Nazareth.

Job faced a chaotic creation run amok by the antics of lawless terrorist powers. Adam came into the world with authority Job did not seem to have: to establish government on the earth to bring order. Jesus came to settle accounts with Satan for the redemption of humanity (Eph. 1:7) and to free the Jews from the bondage to a religious system that should have brought them nearer to God but instead kept them away (Matt. 23:4). At an appointed time in the future every knee in heaven and on earth will bow and confess the supremacy of Jesus (Phil. 2:10). One day the disarming of the powers and principalities because of the cross (Col. 2:15) will be realized. But not today.

Today the cosmic war that allows for no conscientious objectors continues with casualties that are real and tallies that should be unacceptable to a church built upon what Jesus said: "Heal the sick…cast out demons" (Matt. 10:8, nas). At some point numbers matter. While there is anecdotal evidence that some people are healed by the laying on of hands, most are not; otherwise the hospitals would be empty.

While some people are liberated from debilitating spirits through deliverance ministry, many more are not freed. Why does the effectual prayer of righteous people sometimes work and sometimes not? Is the absence of success the reason more churches today than in the past seem reluctant to include healing services as part of their corporate worship? It appears as if many have adopted the maxim of one who wants to build a successful business: stop doing what does not work.

Healing is not simply a matter of having enough faith.

Everyone has watched someone who was full of faith die prematurely of a consuming disease that would not submit to prayer. Of all the infirmities that should be the most responsive to prayer, surely it should be cancer, because its nature is demonic. Cancer occurs when a single cell rebels and creates chaos in a part of the body. Cancer is representative of the original sin of the cosmos—rebellion. If decreeing and declaring the authority of God should subdue any illness, it should be effective against cancer, and yet such is not the usual outcome. What should succeed does not always. Why?

If harnessing evil were simply a matter of prayer, Daniel Pearl would not have been beheaded, nor would the desecrated bodies of the Blackwater contractors been hung from a bridge. If righteous living could safeguard us from a human agent full of evil intent, the Amish schoolchildren would not have been violated and murdered. And yet our belief that prayer *can* and *does* change things is an unalterable tenet of our faith. If prayer empowered by the Holy Spirit cannot restrain the assault of supernatural forces bent on our destruction, then as Paul wrote concerning the resurrection, of all people we Christians are the most foolish. What have we not understood?

WORDS MATTER

Before I worked in television, I was in the movie business. I worked in the acquisition and marketing of major motion picture releases for a large chain of theaters. The man I worked for was a charming eccentric I'll call Bob. Although he was not Jewish, he shared a common belief held by many traditional Jews. Bob believed that words cause reality. He was convinced that speaking certain words, whether good or bad, would cause them to take form and manifest. As a result of how strongly he believed this to be true, certain words could not be uttered in his presence. One day a film representative Bob had known for a long time paid us a call.

"How is your father?" Bob asked.

"Unfortunately, he has developed cancer," the man answered.

To my surprise and that of the visitor, Bob pulled a can of Lysol from his desk and sprayed him with it.

Jewish tradition is not the only religious discipline that teaches how spoken words create reality. Many Christian adherents also hold to some form of this belief, perhaps none more so than Word of Faith followers. Even self-help books such as the New Age–leaning *Think and Grow Rich* by Napoleon Hill insist that thinking about then speaking what one desperately desires to the "universe" will cause all of the forces needed to bring it about to line up and begin moving toward the person with the deep desire.

Hill's book claims: "The universe in which this little earth floats, in which we move and have our being, is itself a form of energy, and it is filled with a form of universal power which adapts itself to the nature of the thoughts we hold in our minds and influences us, in natural ways, to transmute our thoughts into their physical equivalent.... With great emphasis, this power makes no attempt to discriminate between destructive thoughts and constructive thoughts."[1]

Many evangelicals regularly practice the prayer model of declaring and decreeing that certain things will happen. While some might scoff at the idea of creating reality by speaking something into existence, some form of the idea is deeply rooted in the folk culture of America. Almost everyone can recall an instance of having been in conversation with a friend when a third person walked up to hear the friend say, "Speak of the devil."

This is a diminutive form of the original idiom "Speak of the devil and he doth appear." Even people who claim no super-stitious inclinations at all find that there are certain words they are reluctant to speak. It is almost a subconscious guard placed around our words that keeps us from saying particular things that cause us to be anxious or to experience unexplain-able foreboding. Indeed, Scripture cautions us about the con-sequences of language.

> I said, "I will watch my ways and keep my tongue from sin; I will put a muzzle on my mouth as long as the wicked are in my presence."
>
> —Psalm 39:1

> The tongue has the power of life and death.
>
> —Proverbs 18:21

Most Christians are aware of the phenomena known as *glossolalia*, or "speaking in tongues." Also called a "prayer lan-guage," it is the practice of uttering a series of unintelligible sounds as a form of prayer. According to Mark 16:17, Jesus said those who were commissioned to be sent out would be known by certain attributes, one of which would be the ability to speak in new tongues.

There is considerable debate in the modern church as to what Jesus meant and whether speaking in tongues in the Bible was the sudden ability to speak in a language one had not previously known but that was understandable to others, or whether it was an unknown tongue, unintelligible to humans, comprehended only by the Holy Spirit. Paul discounted the former.

> For anyone who speaks in a tongue does not speak to men but to God. Indeed, no one understands him; he utters mysteries with his spirit.
>
> —1 Corinthians 14:2

For our purposes it does not matter which argument is correct. From the beginning of the church age until the present, from time to time people who are otherwise unremarkable in their religious behavior begin to speak in a language they have not been taught and do not understand. The question is, why does it happen?

The argument that the early spread of Christianity relied upon apostles who could speak the languages of the nations they would evangelize, excepting the Day of Pentecost in the Book of Acts, seems a bit hollow. Suppose Paul had visited China and began to speak perfect Mandarin to the people he encountered while he himself had no idea what he was saying. How could he have engaged the people to present the gospel unless he were able to continue to speak the language in ongoing conversation? He says as much in his letter to the church in Corinth.

> So it is with you. Unless you speak intelligible words with your tongue, how will anyone know what you are saying? You will just be speaking into the air.
>
> —1 Corinthians 14:9

We do not see evidence in the New Testament that the apostles acquired the ability to speak in known foreign languages to people as a means of evangelism. Once the practice of charismatic and Pentecostal believers primarily, the ritual of speaking in tongues has become surprisingly mainstream, even among traditional denominations such as the Southern Baptist Convention.

Pastor Dwight McKissic of Cornerstone Baptist Church "triggered the controversial debate within the Southern Baptist Convention on the gifts of the Holy Spirit last year when he spoke of experiencing private prayer language during a chapel service at Southwestern Baptist Theological Seminary. While the majority of Southern Baptist leaders do not practice or accept charismatic practices, Baptists are split on the issue and SBC president Frank Page also recognized and let stand the varying interpretations within the denomination."[2]

Surveys in 2006 estimated that at least 500 million people in the Christian faith worldwide claim to have experienced the phenomena of speaking in unknown tongues while in prayer.[3] Is it ecstatic religious gibberish brought about by spiritual ecstasy—or is it something more? According to the *New York Times* and researchers at the University of Pennsylvania, it appears to fall into the "something more" category. Recent advances in brain scan technology have enabled physicians to observe what occurs in the brain in the midst of religious or meditative practice. By taking brain scans of five women while they were speaking in tongues, remarkable new evidence was observed, as the article states.

Contrary to what may be a common perception, studies suggest that people who speak in tongues rarely suffer from mental problems. A recent study of nearly 1,000 evangelical Christians in England found that those who engaged in the practice were more emotionally stable than those who did not. The new findings contrasted sharply with images taken of other spiritually inspired mental states like meditation, which is often a highly focused mental exercise, activating the frontal lobes.[4]

There is another curious reference to speaking in unknown languages when Paul refers to the tongues of angels (1 Cor. 13:1). What is the native language of angels? How did Paul learn to speak it? Has anyone else ever done it? What if the language of record among celestial beings has something to do with *glossolalia* spoken by humans in prayer?

If God knows our needs without having to be told, why do we need to pray at all? Some may say that we must go through the exercise of prayer because it forms our spiritual character. An improved personality is perhaps a by-product of prayer, but it hardly seems the point. Jesus prayed often, yet it seems doubtful that His character was improved by having done so. Verbal petition to God has within it the power to affect change in the observable world. Jesus said so.

Again, I tell you that if two of you on earth agree about anything you ask for, it will be done for you by my Father in heaven.

—MATTHEW 18:19

Anything? Yet no honest person regardless of faith, maturity, right doctrine, or moral restraint can report that this declaration by Jesus has proven to be completely trustworthy all the time. Sometimes we see the effects of righteous prayer by united intercession, and sometimes we do not. Jesus could have allowed Himself margin for error if He had said, "If two or three of you on earth agree about something you ask for, it might be done for you by My Father if He also agrees. Try it and see." Because words matter, it should tweak our minds that Jesus specifically said, "If two or three of you on *earth* agree." Where else would two or three be located?

Let's suppose that Jesus meant what He said about prayer in agreement with others. What would happen if two groups of equally righteous people were found to be praying in direct opposition to one another about the same thing? Whose prayers would be answered? The Sunday school answer is that the Holy Spirit would decide, and perhaps He would, but there is nothing in Scripture that says this is so.

In the world of math and science the combination of a positive and a negative equals zero. Perhaps in the world of the spirit prayers that are opposed to one another also equal zero—nothing happens; events proceed along whatever paths they were on with neither assistance nor resistance.

A few years ago my husband, Larry, and I owned three houses at the same time: one in Colorado, another in Wisconsin, and another in Florida. We decided that three was too many and we needed to make up our minds where we wanted to live, so we decided to sell the house in Florida because it was the most valuable due to the price of real estate in the boom years of the mid-2000s. We asked our circle of friends in each location to pray the house would sell. They did, but the house did not. Older houses less attractive than ours sold all around us for more money than we were asking. When it had not moved in two years, we changed our plans and sold our lake home in Wisconsin and ultimately the one in Colorado as well.

One day I was sharing with one of our intercessor friends in Florida our confusion about why our house had not sold. She looked at me somewhat sheepishly and said, "To be honest, we were praying that your house would *not* sell because we did not want you to move away." Today, several years later, Larry and I are happy that we have made Florida our home. But the fact remains that prayer in opposition to what we were asking for potentially changed the course of our lives. While things have worked out well for us, there was no guarantee that would be the case. Although the end was not altogether bad, the intercessors prayed in presumption against what they had agreed with us to do.

How many times do you suppose something similar happens when people with contrary agendas pray from the depth of their spirits for different outcomes in the affairs of churches, cities, nations, careers, families, or individuals? What happens when one group prays for mercy and another prays for judgment? What happens when the farmers pray it rains and the vacationers pray it does not? In the mechanical world, a positive and a negative equal zero. In the spiritual world, it equals chaos.

Perhaps Jesus set a low mark for how many were needed to bring about God's movement in our world because He knew how difficult it would be to get two or three self-righteous entities to agree on anything. It is also why Paul tells us to pray unceasingly in the spirit (Eph. 6:18; 1 Thess. 5:17). Petitioning in an unknown tongue is the means God has given to insure His will gets prayed whether we are conscious of what we are saying or not. How much evil could be restrained if there were not so much disagreement as to how and what to pray for? I have known people who will not allow hands to be laid on them because they have learned that a curse can sometimes masquerade as a prayer.

BEWARE THE PRAYERS OF BINDING AND LOOSING

God is not a legalist, but Satan and all who are aligned with him are. Words create reality. Before anything that exists *was*, someone spoke the word that described it. Every building, every discovery, every piece of technology was a word in someone's mouth before it became real. In the beginning of anything there was first the word. People of prayer ought to be much more mindful of the casual use of powerful spiritual language than they often are.

A couple of years ago I was part of a prayer meeting at Covenant Centre International in Palm Beach Gardens, Florida, where I am currently a pastor and teacher. It was a common practice for intercessors to pray aloud for the binding of evil spirits and loosing of God's blessing. After the meeting a new friend named Tom Mansmith, formerly an Assembly of God pastor who now works for the American Cancer Society, stopped me on my way out.

"You may want to rethink encouraging the intercessors to pray binding and loosing prayers so freely over this church," he said. When I asked why, he went on to say, "Binding and loosing may not mean what you think it does." (A complete study of these terms can be found at tommansmithministries .com.)

I admit that at the moment I tended to dismiss Tom's caution. After all, what is there to know? The idea of binding and loosing is one Jesus told His disciples about.

> I will give you the keys of the kingdom of heaven; whatever you bind on earth will be bound in heaven, and whatever you loose on earth will be loosed in heaven.
>
> —MATTHEW 16:19

The next day I found I could not stop thinking about Tom's words. So another pastoral colleague and I invited Tom to come into the church to explain his concerns. After listening to a perspective I had never before considered and following up on the study, I have become convinced that when we begin to use spiritual terms designed to harness or release supernatural powers...forgive us, Father, for we know not what we do.

The disciples would have been familiar with the term "bind" from the Old Testament.

> You shall bind them as a sign on your hand and they shall be as frontals on your forehead.
>
> —DEUTERONOMY 6:8, NAS

> You shall therefore impress these words of mine on your heart and on your soul; and you shall bind them as a sign on your hand, and they shall be as frontals on your forehead.
>
> —DEUTERONOMY 11:18, NAS

> Do not let kindness and truth leave you; bind them around your neck.
>
> —PROVERBS 3:3, NAS

The word *bind* is the Greek word *deo*. It means to fasten one thing to another, often with chains. The following example of usage is from Vine's lexicon: "A woman who was bent together, had been 'bound' by Satan through the work of a demon (Luke 13:16)."[5]

In other words, in the Old Testament and in the common understanding in the first century, when one used the word *bind*, it was understood to be in reference to tightly fastening something to oneself. Jennifer Cobb, writing for the World Network of Prayer, explains it like this.

> The word "bind" literally means to under gird, heal, hold, persuade, steady, cause fragmented pieces to come back into one whole, put oneself under obligation; cling to. When you obey the words of the Lord by binding and loosing, you are bringing your life into alignment. Binding prayers stabilize you....
>
>> "Lord, I bind my mind to the mind of Christ so that I can have the thoughts and feelings of your heart in me." (Philippians 2:5, Romans 12:2)
>>
>> "I bind my will to the will of Christ. Align my will with yours." (Matthew 6:10)
>>
>> "I bind my emotions to you, oh Lord, so that I can have stability in my life."
>>
>> "Lord, I bind myself to the cross."[6]

With this understanding in mind, what do you suppose might happen when an intercessor calls out directly to a demonic spirit such as lust with the words, "I bind you and all your manifestations in Jesus's name"? He may have inadvertently tightly fastened the spirit to himself, bringing about the exact opposite effect he intended. Over the years I have known hundreds of intercessors, and I have often been concerned as to why so many of them seem to suffer from the very kinds of spiritual attacks they are supposed to ward off. *What you whistle for will come.* Ignorance of the law does not lessen its consequences. Our intentions may not matter if we apply a spiritual law in the wrong way. A story I once heard about the settling of the American West is an illustration.

The lore goes that a wagon train was crossing the barren land between Fort Stockton, Texas, and El Paso when a group of Native Americans attacked it. In the battle the natives captured a box of loaded rifles and drug it outside the circled wagons. When they opened the box and grabbed the weapons, they launched a fresh assault against the settlers. Yet not a single settler was shot. The Indians knew guns were weapons but had never been taught to use them, so they applied the knowledge they had of other armaments. They grabbed the rifles by the barrels and swung the butts like clubs at the settlers. Many times during the fight the rifles accidentally discharged, shooting the one who was wielding it.

If we were wrong about *binding*, are we wrong about *loosing* as well? Probably. The Greek word *luo* means to loose, to release, to dissolve, annul, break up, or destroy. Or, as Cobb wrote, "To 'loose' means to untie, break up, destroy, dissolve, melt, put off, wreck, crack to sunder by separation of the parts, shatter into minute fragments, disrupt, lacerate, break forth, burst, rend and tear up."[7]

Therefore, if we loose the spirit of prosperity in our midst, what are we actually praying will happen? If we use Cobb's definition, we may be wrecking, shattering, putting off, and tearing up the blessings of riches that might have otherwise been coming our way.

HOW ARE WE TO USE THESE TERMS?

In terms of containing demonic strategies, we are not to use these words at all. We can only understand what Jesus meant if we look at the context. Before He mentioned binding and loosing, He first said something else.

> Jesus replied, "Blessed are you, Simon son of Jonah, for this was not revealed to you by man, but by my Father in heaven. And I tell you that you are Peter, and on this rock I will build my church, and the gates of Hades will not overcome it."
>
> —MATTHEW 16:17–18

When Jesus told Peter that what he bound on earth would be bound in heaven, He was talking about how the government of the church would be established. In other words, "Peter, upon your confession of who I am I will build My church. And concerning the church, what you legislate as policy on the earth, I will back up in heaven."

Fathers of evangelicalism such as John Wesley and Matthew Henry agreed that what Jesus meant in telling Peter that what he bound on earth would be bound in heaven was intended to allow for a change of rules from Judaism to how the church of the new covenant would function. For example, when Peter heard from God in Acts 10 that no foods were unclean and that uncircumcised Gentiles were worthy of the baptism of the Holy Spirit in equality with the Jews, Peter's acceptance and affirmation of this new revelation wiped out half of the rules of Leviticus. When the council in Jerusalem in Acts 15 ratified what Peter and also Paul decreed about the Gentiles, the rules previously written in heaven and handed down to mankind shifted and aligned with the rule of the apostles on the earth.

Similar actions by the church over the centuries are easily documented. Under the guidance of the Holy Spirit the church came to recognize that it should no longer forbid women to serve in ministry, prohibit divorce and remarriage, or ban long hair on men and short hair on women. What the church bound on earth was bound in heaven, and what it loosed on earth was loosed in heaven. The church changed its mind, and heaven stood in agreement with the church. This is how over the centuries the church has legitimately instituted change.

We no longer think it is a good idea to sell one's daughter into slavery or to kill a man for hauling wood on the Sabbath. The church of the new covenant legislated change from the old covenant, and heaven backed it up. The extraordinarily good news is that as new revelation continues to come from the Holy Spirit about things we previously did not understand or were simply wrong about, such as whether getting a tattoo, wearing two types of cloth at the same time, and dabbling in the occult ought to carry the same penalty, the church can change its position yet again. This is profound.

Using the principles of binding and loosing as a means of

controlling the activities of supernatural powers is a misapplication of a powerful principle that produces unexpected consequences. Clichés become such because they are widely spoken truth. "Be careful what you pray for, you might get it" is not a flippant response to overly ambitious prayer. It is a genuine warning to proceed with caution. If you think it and repeatedly say it, you are likely to get it—whether you meant it or not.

Chapter 14

AND MY POINT IS?

THIS IS NOT a book I planned to write. Said more honestly, it is a book I purposely planned *not* to write. I am much more at ease in the world of fiction and fantasy, where ideas can be explored and possibilities offered without the burden of facts or the consequences of causing someone to believe something that may be interesting but wrong.

After completing a fiction series titled the Reluctant Demon

Diaries, a colleague persisted in challenging me to write a nonfiction book about angels and demons. That assignment alone would have been an ambitious undertaking. When I asked why he thought such a book would be of interest, he surprised me with his answer: "Because you should tell people what they do not know about Lucifer." The natural follow-up question from a rational person would have been, "Whatever would make you think I know something like that?" I am not sure why I did not ask it.

Not convinced it was a good idea, I wrote a few pages and circulated them among an inner circle of friends and pastors whose spiritual insight I value. All strongly felt I should pursue the project. Over the months I have been researching and writing, my friends have maintained vigilant prayer that if the Holy Spirit wanted to say something different to the church through this book, I would have ears to hear it. Each week someone called to check on me to inquire how the writing was going.

Every author will tell you that once a book is begun it writes itself, sometimes in a completely different direction than the author originally planned. When I was writing the fourth book of the Reluctant Demon Diaries, *The Redeemer*, it was widely anticipated by readers of the first three books that a number of complex theological conundrums would have to be resolved. I received hundreds of e-mails asking how it would all work out in the end. I remember thinking, "I cannot wait to find out myself. I will not know until I write it."

As this book began to reveal itself, I found it increasingly difficult to give a simple answer to "how is the writing going?" I mumbled a few vague comments about it being more complex than I planned and that I was not sure where I was in the process. As the deadline for turning in the manuscript to the publisher neared and my colleagues became somewhat concerned about my progress, Lana, a trusted friend of many years, asked a direct question.

"Is this book about anything?" she said.

"Yes, of course it is," I answered. "What do you mean?"

"It sounds like you are doing a lot of research, and we are wondering if there is a point in there somewhere."

Well, yes, there is, and since this is the last chapter, I suppose it is time to make it, though I confess some reluctance to doing so and have spent several days trying to come up with an alternative ending that would be less controversial than the one I will offer here. Since I intentionally shared the manuscript with very few people prior to publication, there are no particular expectations for how it should conclude, so there is still time to write a hasty summation and assure readers that it all works out just fine in the end, which I am confident it will. The problem is, we are nowhere close to the end.

The genesis of this book did not really begin with my colleague's suggestion to write it. It began more than a dozen years ago when I found myself frustrated with God about His lack of attention to the plight of the righteous. It was the year after we sold our television station in Minnesota and found ourselves heavily involved with a number of ministries crossing several denominational lines. While things were going well for us, this was not the case in the lives of some of the most faithful people I have ever encountered. It was the year I knew, as Brian McLaren once said of his own circumstances, that I was caught between something real and something wrong. It was also the year I had the dream.

The prior ten years of my life in broadcasting had been very public and filled with examples of the goodness of the Lord during times of uncertainty and challenge. My new assignment was to be president of a private foundation. I also taught adult Bible education in a Lutheran church and occasionally at the Lutheran Association of Renewed Churches. I also taught an additional class weekly at a prophetic school of ministry and led a Sunday night charismatic praise and worship service called River of God. As a result I was frequently involved in powerful prayer services in several ministries and churches. In so many ways those were the most spiritually fulfilling years of my life.

Except for the people who died—tragic losses of people too young to succumb to the devastating illnesses that came without provocation and would not submit to prayer or deliverance. Holy people, who believed they would be healed but were not. Powerful prayers from seasoned and anointed ministers who banged on the doors of heaven for healing, yet healing did not come.

I rejected then, as now, the cliché that death is the ultimate healing. If that were so, Jesus would not have said, "Heal the sick, raise the dead...cast out demons" (Matt. 10:8, NAS). Jesus overcame the grip of death, but premature demise is not in God's plan for anyone, nor is it a blessing for parents to bury their children.

I soon learned that while I had been a very good television executive, I was terrible at being a professional minister. It was not that other ministers around me were having better results; it was simply that I did not have the faith to continue assuring people of something I could see was not true. Something was not right, but I did not know what it was. If we were indeed conquerors and a victorious church, as the Bible proclaims, why were we seeing so few results? I pleaded with God to show me how tragic human loss and devastation would someday be understood in the greater plan of eternal glory.

"I do not have to know it all," I prayed. "Just show me how any of this will somehow make sense for eternity."

Soon after is when I had the dream. It was a picture of eternity all right, but not as I expected. It was a vision of eternity past, not future. I am somewhat reluctant to offer my dream as a reason why any person should be influenced by revelation I might have received, because I am acutely aware that most cults and false religions began as a result of someone having a dream or an angelic visitation that could not be verified by anyone else. There are, however, also dreams by individuals that have shaped our faith, such as Paul's Damascus road experience, or that even changed our faith, such as Peter's dream in Acts 10 of a sheet being let down from heaven filled with animals long considered unclean. Only the passage of time clarifies what kind of dream or visitation it truly is.

Although it was dramatic, particularly as I seemed to see and understand how things were before the cosmic rebellion occurred, it still did not address the issues that had led me to pray in the first place. So I thanked God for the revelation but added that it had not helped me to understand why horrible things were happening to people who had done nothing to deserve them and why prayer seemed so ineffective to bring relief. It may be important to add that at the time I was beginning an end-time study on the Book of Revelation.

"Why did You show me this dream?" I prayed.

I do not know that I heard an audible voice; probably not. While I am not sure how the answer came, I know with certainty that it did. I understood God to say, "I showed you this because you cannot understand the end until you understand the beginning." I will not pretend to have comprehended what this meant. Over time I found myself asking more questions about what I heard so clearly in the spirit. *The end of what? The earth? Humanity? The age?*

Perhaps you know what it is like to be haunted by a verse of Scripture. After my dream the verse that began to frequent and even trouble my thoughts is from the Gospel of Matthew, one for which I can find no suitable resolution in all the commentaries I have searched. "As it was in the days of Noah, so it will be at the coming of the Son of Man" (Matt. 24:37).

When I began my serious study of Revelation, like many Christians who form their beliefs more from conferences and religious television than from seminary or disciplined research, I tried to use the Mount Olivet discourse from Matthew 24 as a marker for the return of Jesus. When I began an academic study, I learned that Jesus was mostly prophesying about the fall of Jerusalem, where all but one of His predictions did ultimately happen, not about the second coming to earth. The only marker Jesus mentioned that could not easily be attributed to some other point in history was the verse that haunted me: *As it was in the days of Noah...*

Not the eating, drinking, or marrying part, which has been

true of every generation and against which there is no law. He must have meant something else. The first-century Jews knew what He meant, but it has been largely lost to Western civilization. This is the long-promised point of this book.

The cosmos is much more complicated than we think it is, filled with highly advanced, self-willed celestial beings, some of whom view humanity as prey. These beings frequently transgress their assigned borders and wreak havoc on the earth and all its inhabitants. At an appointed time in the future Jesus will return; then reconciliation and justice will be brought to bear on all who have warred against God and His creation, whether things in heaven or on earth (Col. 1:19–20). *Reconciliation* does not necessarily mean redemption, and *justice* does not necessarily mean punishment. Jesus alone will define those terms. But before this happens, wickedness will increase. Violence will increase. Demonic powers will become more brazen in their trespasses. Why does Luke 21:23 say how dreadful it will be for *pregnant* women? Why not all women?

Stephen Hawking—celebrated physicist, self-acknowledged atheist, author of *A Brief History of Time*, and heralded as the world's smartest man—was asked if he believed in aliens and if he thought they would ever visit our planet.

"If aliens ever visit us," he answered, "the outcome would be much as when Columbus landed in America, which didn't turn out well for the Native Americans."[1]

Before the Son of Man comes, *as it was in the days of Noah* (Matt. 24:37), mankind will be eating, drinking, and marrying (v. 38), unaware that it will soon find itself engaged in a war against an enemy it did not anticipate. God says, "My people are destroyed from lack of knowledge" (Hosea 4:6). It will find itself battling an earthbound race that God did not intend and for whom there is no place in heaven or the earth— the Nephilim. It is a dreadful foe only the victorious church is authorized to combat.

"But when these things begin to take place, straighten up and lift up your heads, because your redemption is drawing near" (Luke 21:28, NAS). In that day 1 Thessalonians 5 assures us that the people of God will not be overcome: "But you, brethren, are not in darkness, that the day would overtake you like a thief; for you are all sons of light and sons of day. We are not of night nor of darkness; so then let us not sleep as others do, but let us be alert and sober" (vv. 4–6, NAS).

Let us as believers be like the sons of Isacchar and understand the times we are living in and what "the church" ought to do. Let us arise with spiritual swords more sharply honed, with more understanding of the tactics of the supernatural world, and armed with informed, fervent, unceasing prayer as the manifold wisdom of God is at last made known through the triumphant church to the powers and principalities in heavenly places as the holy angels and the prayers of the saints unite.

> When the Lamb broke the seventh seal, there was silence in heaven for about half an hour. And I saw the seven angels who stand before God, and seven trumpets were given to them. Another angel came and stood at the altar, holding a golden censer; and much incense was given to him, so that he might add it to the prayers of all the saints on the golden altar which was before the throne. And the smoke of the incense, with the prayers of the saints, went up

before God out of the angel's hand. Then the angel took the censer and filled it with the fire of the altar, and threw it to the earth; and there followed peals of thunder and sounds and flashes of lightning and an earthquake. And the seven angels who had the seven trumpets prepared themselves to sound them.

—Revelation 8:1–6

Before Jesus returns, it will be as it was in the days of Noah. The church's finest hour is coming.

Notes

CHAPTER 1
MORE QUESTIONS THAN ANSWERS

1. Associated Press, "Albany, N.Y. Mail Carrier Saves Baby Falling From Window," April 22, 2008, http://www.usatoday.com/news/nation/2008-04-22-3132818466_x.htm (accessed April 4, 2012).

2. David Kocieniewski and Gary Gately, "Man Shoots 11, Killing 5 Girls, in Amish School," New *York Times*, October 3, 2006, http://www.nytimes.com/2006/10/03/us/03amish.html?_r=1&pagewanted=all (accessed April 4, 2012).

3. John Calvin, *Institutes of the Christian Religion*, vol. 1, ed. John T. McNeill (Louisville, KY: Westminster John Knox Press, 1973), 199. Viewed at Google Books.

4. Colin Freeman, "Horror at Fallujah," *San Francisco Chronicle*, April 1, 2004, http://www.sfgate.com/cgi-bin/article.cgi?f=/c/a/2004/04/01/MNGH35UO801.DTL&ao=all (accessed April 4, 2012).

5. Brother Lawrence, *The Practice of the Presence of God*, trans. John J. Delaney (Garden City, NY: Image, 1977), 95–96, 100, as quoted in Gregory A. Boyd, *Satan and the Problem of Evil* (Downers Grove, IL: InterVarsity Press, 2001), 13. Viewed at Google Books.

6. Frank Pellegrini, "Daniel Pearl: 1963–2002," *Time*, February 21, 2002, http://www.time.com/time/nation/article/0,8599,212284,00.html (accessed April 4, 2012).

7. Rory McCarthy, "Body Parts Believed to Be of Murdered US Reporter," *The Guardian*, May 17, 2002, http://www.guardian.co.uk/media/2002/may/18/pressandpublishing.pakistan (accessed April 4, 2012).

8. E. Frank Tupper, *Scandalous Providence: The Jesus Story of the Compassion of God* (Macon, GA: Mercer University Press, 1995), 60.

9. Boyd, *Satan and the Problem of Evil*, 15.

CHAPTER 2
WHEN WAR BROKE OUT IN HEAVEN

1. Rabbi Nosson Scherman, *The Stone Edition Chumash*, ninth edition (Brooklyn, NY: Mesorah Publications, 1998).

2. Boyd, *Satan and the Problem of Evil*, 30.

3. "Lexical Aids to the Old Testament," *Hebrew-Greek Key Word Study Bible*, New American Standard (Chattanooga, TN: AMG Publishers, 2008).

CHAPTER 3
THE DISTURBING CASE OF JOB

1. Edmond Jacob, *Theology of the Old Testament* (New York: Harper & Row, 1958), 171.

2. *Hebrew-Greek Key Word Study Bible*, New American Standard, 669.

3. Christopher M. Rios, "Claiming Complementarity: Twentieth-Century Evangelical Applications of an Idea," *Perspectives on Science and Christian Faith* 63, no. 2 (June 2011): 75–84, http://www.asa3.org/ASA/PSCF/2011/PSCF6-11Rios .pdf (accessed June 4, 2012).

4. Ibid., 78, referencing Donald M. MacKay, "Persons and Things," in *Science and Faith Today* (London: Lutterworth Press, 1953), 33–35.

5. Ibid., citing Donald M. MacKay, "Looking for Connections," in James B. Torrance et al., *Where Science and Brain Meet* (London: InterVarsity Fellowship, 1953), 17.

6. Stephen S. Hall, "Last of the Neanderthals," *National Geographic,* October 2008, http://ngm.nationalgeographic.com/print/2008/10/neanderthals/hall-text (accessed April 5, 2012).

7. Ibid.

8. Arthur Khachatryan, "Scientific Insights From the Oldest Book of the Bible," *Cold and Lonely Truth* (blog), January 31, 2012, http://www.cltruth.com/blog/2012/scientific-insights -from-oldest-book-the-bible/, accessed May 18, 2012.

CHAPTER 4
THE WATCHERS

1. J. Stephen Lang, *1,001 Things You Always Wanted to Know About Angels, Demons, and the Afterlife* (Nashville: Thomas Nelson, 2000), 487.

2. Graham Hancock, *Fingerprints of the Gods* (New York: Three Rivers Press, 1995), 135.

3. Ibid., 135.

4. Patrick Heron, *The Nephilim and the Pyramid of the Apocalypse* (Maitland, FL: Xulon Press, 2005), 81.

5. Gregory A. Boyd, *God at War* (Downers Grove, IL: InterVarsity Press, 2001), 178.

6. Catholic.org, "St. Anthony of Padua: Doctor of the Church," http://www.catholic.org/saints/saint.php?saint_id=24 (accessed June 4, 2012).

7. Catholic.org, "St. Fiacre," http://www.catholic.org/saints/saint.php?saint_id=276 (accessed June 4, 2012).

8. Catholic.org, "St. Adalbert of Prague," http://www
.catholic.org/saints/saint.php?saint_id=858 (accessed June 4,
2012).

9. Catholic.org, "St. Angsar," http://www.catholic.org/saints/
saint.php?saint_id=257 (accessed June 4, 2012).

10. Catholic.org, "St. Vincent de Paul," http://www.catholic
.org/saints/saint.php?saint_id=326 (accessed June 4, 2012).

11. As quoted in Boyd, *God at War*, 136.

12. James Kallas, *The Significance of the Synoptic Miracles*
(Eugene, OR: Wipf and Stock Publishers, 2010), 78, as quoted
in Boyd, *God at War*, 186.

13. Boyd, *God at War*, 186.

14. Bill Bryson, *A Short History of Nearly Everything* (New
York: Broadway Books, 2003), 24–25.

15. Ibid., 143.

16. Ibid., 144.

17. Ibid., 145.

18. Kevin Bonsor and Robert Lamb, "How Time Travel
Works," HowStuffWorks.com, http://science.howstuffworks
.com/science-vs-myth/everyday-myths/time-travel.htm (accessed
June 6, 2012).

CHAPTER 5
THE DAUGHTERS OF MEN

1. Boyd, *God at War*, 138.

2. Chuck Missler, "Mischievous Angels or Sethites?", Koinoinia House, http://www.khouse.org/articles/1997/110/ (accessed June 6, 2012).

3. J. Karst Eusebus-Werke, *Die Chronik*, vol. 5, Leipzig, 1911, as quoted in Patrick Heron, *The Nephilim and the Pyramid of the Apocalypse* (New York: Kensington Publishing Company, 2004), 65.

4. Enoch 7:1–6, Sacred-Texts.com, http://www.sacred-texts .com/bib/boe/boe010.htm (accessed June 5, 2012).

5. Homer, *The Iliad*, book 8, translated by Samuel Butler, http://classics.mit.edu/Homer/iliad.8.viii.html (accessed June 5, 2012).

6. Richard Rohr, "Jesus as Liberator," St. Joseph's Catholic Church–Cedara," August 20, 2011, http://www.stjocedara .org.za/Jesus-as-Liberator.html (accessed June 5, 2012).

7. N. T. Wright, *Paul* (Minneapolis, MN: Fortress Press, 2009), 120–122.

8. Biblos.com, "3045. *yada*," http://concordances .org/hebrew/3045.htm (accessed June 5, 2012).

9. Biblos.com, "2087. *heteros*," http://concordances .org/greek/2087.htm (accessed June 5, 2012).

10. Biblos.com, "4561. *sarx*," http://concordances .org/greek/4561.htm (accessed June 5, 2012).

11. John E. Mack, *Abduction: Human Encounters With Aliens* (New York: Ballantine Books, 1994), 411, as referenced in Michael Tummillo, "Alien Invasion of Planet Earth, Part One," Ezinearticles.com, http://ezinearticles.com/?Alien-Invasion-of -Planet-Earth-PART-ONE&id=60415 (accessed June 5, 2012).

12. C. D. B. Bryan, *Close Encounters of the Fourth Kind: Alien Abduction, UFOs, and the Conference at M.I.T.* (New York: Random House Digital, 2011). Viewed at Google Books.

CHAPTER 6
JESUS—SON OF AN ANGEL?

1. Sayyid Rida Akrami, "What Is Known About Jesus Christ?", Aabid Waqar, trans., *Islam Times*, January 8, 2011, http://islamtimes.org/vdcc4pq0.2bqop8y-a2.html (accessed June 5, 2012).

2. Abul Kasem, "Allah Plays With His Souls, Part 2," Islam-watch.org, October 29, 2008, http://www.islam-watch .org/AbulKasem/Allah-Plays-with-His-Souls2.htm (accessed June 5, 2012).

3. Cathy Lynn Grossman, "Bishops Boot 'Booty' From Revised Bible," *USA Today*, March 2, 2011, http://www .usatoday.com/news/religion/2011-03-02-1Abible02_ST_N.htm (accessed June 5, 2012).

Chapter 7
Why Did Jesus Establish the Church?

1. *Microsoft Encarta College Dictionary* (New York: St. Martin's Press, 2001), s.v. "religion." Viewed at Google Books.

2. StudyLight.org, "Holman Bible Dictionary: Caesarea Phillipi," http://www.studylight.org/dic/hbd/view .cgi?number=T1100 (accessed June 5, 2012).

3. John Paul Jackson, *Needless Casualties of War* (Nashville: Streams Publications, 1999), 49.

4. Boyd, *God at War*, 182.

5. Ibid., 184.

6. Malachi Martin, *Hostage to the Devil* (San Francisco: Harper Collins, 1992), xvii,

7. Jackson, *Needless Casualties of War*, 82.

8. Martin, *Hostage to the Devil*, xx.

9. Ibid., 13.

10. Ibid., xxiii.

11. Doris Wagner, e-mail communication with the author, July 20, 2011.

12. Ibid.

Chapter 8
Lesser Gods

1. Justin Martyr, "Chapter V.—How the Angels Transgressed," *The Apostolic Fathers With Justin Martyr and Irenaeus,*

Christian Classics Ethereal Library, http://www.ccel.org/ccel/
schaff/anf01.viii.iii.v.html (accessed June 6, 2012).

2. N. T. Wright, *The New Testament and the People of God*
(n.p.: Fortress Press, 1992), 258.

3. Boyd, *God at War*, 121.

4. Adele Berlin, Marc Zvi Brettler, and Michael Fishbane,
*The Jewish Study Bible: featuring The Jewish Publication Society
TANAKH Translation* (New York: Oxford University Press,
2004), s.v. "Gen. 2.25–3.1a."

5. BlueLetterBible.org, "Vine's Expository Dictionary of
New Testament Words: Strong's Number G3439, *Monogenes*,"
http://www.blueletterbible.org/Search/Dictionary/viewTopic
.cfm?type=getTopic&Topic=Only+Begotten&DictID=9#Vines
(accessed June 6, 2012).

Chapter 9
The Weapons of Warfare—
Proceed With Caution

1. Barbara Yoder, in correspondence with the author, September 2011.

2. Leanne Payne, *Listening Prayer* (Grand Rapids, MI:
Baker Book House, 1999), 67.

3. Jackson, *Needless Casualties of War*, 35.

4. M. Scott Peck, *The People of the Lie* (New York: Touch-
stone Books, 1983, 1998), 28.

5. Ibid., 30–31.

6. Lausanne.org, "The Lausanne Covenant: 12. Spiritual Conflict," The Lausanne Movement, http://www.lausanne.org/en/documents/lausanne-covenant.html (accessed June 6, 2012).

7. Lausanne.org, "The Manila Manifesto," The Lausanne Movement, http://www.lausanne.org/en/documents/manila-manifesto.html (accessed June 6, 2012).

8. Lausanne.org, "Statement on Spiritual Warfare (1993)," The Lausanne Movement, http://www.lausanne.org/en/documents/all/consultation-statements/206-statement-on-spiritual-warfare-1993.html (accessed June 5, 2012).

9. Lausanne.org, "Deliver Us From Evil: Consultation Statement," The Lausanne Movement, August 2000, http://www.lausanne.org/no/component/content/article.html?id=179 (accessed June 6, 2012).

10. Ibid.

11. Ibid.

12. Claire Gordon, "The Rise of the Religious Left," HuffingtonPost.com, June 19, 2011, http://www.huffingtonpost.com/claire-gordon/the-rise-of-the-religious_b_879137.html (accessed June 6, 2012).

CHAPTER 10
SOMETHING WICKED THIS WAY COMES

1. Jason Beaubien, "Against a Scarred Landscape, Haitians Persevere," NPR.org, January 5, 2011, http://www.npr.org/2011/01/05/132657376/against-a-scarred-landscape-haitians-persevere (accessed June 6, 2012).

2. Alexei Barrionuevo and Liz Robbins, "1.5 Million Displaced After Chile Quake," *New York Times*, February 27, 2010, http://www.nytimes.com/2010/02/28/world/americas/28chile .html?pagewanted=all (accessed June 6, 2012).

3. Associated Press, "Earthquake-Weary Christchurch Rattled by New Quake," CBC News, June 13, 2011, http://www .cbc.ca/news/world/story/2011/06/12/new-zealand-earthquake -christchurch-collapse.html (accessed June 6, 2012).

4. Barbara Demick, David Pierson, and Kenji Hall, "8.9 Quake Kills Hundreds in Japan," *Los Angeles Times*, March 11, 2011, http://articles.latimes.com/2011/mar/11/world/ la-fg-japan-quake-20110311 (accessed June 6, 2012).

5. Michael K. Tippett, Adam H. Sobel, and Suzana J. Camargo, "Association of U.S. Tornado Counts With the Large-Scale Environment on Monthly Time-Scales," *Science and Technology Infusion Climate Bulletin*, October 3–6, 2011, http://www.nws.noaa.gov/ost/climate/STIP/36CDPW/ 36cdpw-mtippett2.pdf (accessed June 6, 2012).

6. Ibid.

7. Associated Press, "2011 Tornado Outbreak Death Toll Hits 337, Second-Deadliest Day From Twister in U.S. History," *Huffington Post*, June 29, 2011, http://www.huffingtonpost .com/2011/04/30/2011-tornado-outbreak-deaths _n_855646.html (accessed June 6, 2012).

8. Associated Press, "Death Toll Rises to 132 After Joplin, Missouri, Tornado," KCRG.com, May 27, 2011, http://www .kcrg.com/news/local/Midwest-Cleaning-up-After-Weekend

-Severe-Weather-Outbreak-122425159.html (accessed June 6, 2012).

9. John Hick, *Evil and the God of Love* (New York: Harper & Row, 1978), 12.

10. Boyd, *Satan and the Problem of Evil*, 247.

11. Martin Luther, *Luther's Works*, vol. 54 (n.p.: Concordia Publishing House, 1986), 82. Viewed at Google Books.

12. C. Peter Wagner, "Some Personal Thoughts About Japan for Informed Intercession," ElijahList.com, March 20, 2011, http://www.elijahlist.com/words/display_word_pf.html?ID=9742 (accessed June 7, 2012).

13. Ibid.

14. Ibid.

15. Wikipedia.org, s.v. "Enthronement of the Japanese Emperor," http://en.wikipedia.org/wiki/Enthronement_of_the_Japanese_Emperor#The_Daijo-sai (accessed June 7, 2012).

16. Wagner, "Some Personal Thoughts About Japan for Informed Intercession."

17. Mark Twain, "Letter VII," *Letters From the Earth* (New York: Fawcett Crest Books, 1966), 34. Viewed at Google Books.

18. Athenagoras, "A Plea for Christianity," as quoted in Boyd, *Satan and the Problem of Evil*, 294.

19. Origen, *Against Celsus* 8, as quoted in Boyd, *Satan and the Problem of Evil*, 294.

20. Jackson, *Needless Casualties of War*, 49.

21. Peter T. O'Brien, *Colossians, Philemon*, Word Biblical Commentary, vol. 44 (Nashville: Word Books, 1982), 114.

22. C. Peter Wagner, *Warfare Prayer* (Shippensburg, PA: Destiny Image, 2009), 208–209.

23. John Bechtle, "What Is the Job Description for an Angel?", in ChristianAnswers.net, "What Does the Bible Teach About Angels?", http://christiananswers.net/q-acb/acb-t005.html (accessed June 6, 2012).

24. St. Gregory, *Homily 34: In Evang.*, in NewAvent.org, The Catholic Encyclopedia, s.v. "angels," http://www.newadvent.org/cathen/01476d.htm (accessed June 7, 2012).

Chapter 11
A Slippery Slope—a Word of Caution

1. Boyd, *God at War*, 204.

2. OpusAngelorum.org, "Brief History of Opus Angelorum and Its Development Within the Church," http://opusangelorum.org/about-us/brief_history.html (accessed June 7, 2012).

3. CatholicCulture.org, "Decree on the Doctrine and Customs of the Association 'Opus Angelorum,'" http://www.catholicculture.org/culture/library/view.cfm?recnum=7938 (accessed June 7, 2012).

4. Ibid.

5. Ibid.

6. Ibid.

7. Zenit.org, "Doctrinal Congregation's Note on Opus Angelorum," http://www.zenit.org/article-30858?l=english (accessed June 7, 2012).

8. *The Week*, "Vatican Warns Bishops on Angel-Worshipping Sect," November 5, 2010, http://www.theweek.co.uk/politics /10157/vatican-warns-bishops-angel-worshipping-sect (accessed June 7, 2012).

9. Vatican Radio, "CDF on the Status of Opus Angelorum," http://storico.radiovaticana.org/en1/storico/2010-11/436378_ cdf_on_the_status_of_opus_angelorum.html (accessed June 7, 2012).

10. Ibid.

11. "Those Who See the Face of God," originally published in the weekly English edition of L'Osservatore Romano (Vatican newspaper), March 23, 2011, OpusAngelorum.org, http://www .opusangelorum.org/English/OA_LOsservatore/OA_spirituality .htm (accessed June 6, 2012).

CHAPTER 12
CAN FALLEN ANGELS BE REDEEMED?

1. *Adam Clarke's Commentary*, electronic database, copyright © 1996 by Biblesoft.

2. One-Heaven.org, "Frequently Asked Questions," http:// one-heaven.org/content/faq_general.html (accessed June 7, 2012).

3. One-Heaven.org, "Covenant of One Heaven," Article 1: Purpose of Covenant, http://one-heaven.org/covenant/article/1 .html (accessed June 7, 2012).

CHAPTER 13
YOU WILL HAVE WHAT YOU SAY

1. Napoleon Hill, *Think and Grow Rich* (Chula Vista, CA:_ Aventine Press, 2008), 20–21.

2. Audrey Barrick, "Southern Baptists Debate Over Speaking in Tongues," *The Christian Post*, May 1, 2007, http:// www.christianpost.com/news/southern-baptists-debate -over-speaking-in-tongues-27177/ (accessed June 7, 2012).

3. The Pew Forum on Religion and Public Life, *Spirit and Power: A 10-Country Survey of Pentecostals*, Washington DC, October 2006, http://www.pewforum.org/uploadedfiles/ Orphan_Migrated_Content/pentecostals-08.pdf (accessed June 7, 2012).

4. Benedict Carey, "A Neuroscientific Look at Speaking in Tongues," *New York Times*, November 7, 2006, http://www .nytimes.com/2006/11/07/health/07brain.html (accessed June 7, 2012).

5. *Vine's Expository Dictionary of New Testament Words* (Nashville: Thomas Nelson, 1985), s.v. "bind, binding," electronic database, copyright © 1996 by Biblesoft.

6. Jennifer Cobb, "Binding and Loosing," World Network of Prayer, February 1, 2009, http://wnop.org/index.php?option

=com_content&view=article&id=186:binding-and-loosing-& catid=75:personal-prayer&Itemid=164 (accessed June 7, 2012).

7. Ibid.

Chapter 14
And My Point Is?

1. Ki Mae Heussner, "Stephen Hawking: Alien Contact Could Be Risky," ABCNews.com, April 26, 2010, http:// abcnews.go.com/Technology/Space/stephen-hawking-alien -contact-risky/story?id=10478157#.T80BQLBYtT4 (accesed June 7, 2012).